Hunting the
Long-tailed Bird

Hunting the Long-tailed Bird
by Bob Bell

799.242
B413h

FRESHET PRESS Rockville Center, New York

Copyright   1975 by Freshet Press

All rights reserved. Brief quotations from this book may be used in newspaperxxxxxxx

Copyright © 1975 by Freshet Press

All rights reserved. Brief quotations from this book may be used in newspaper or magazine reviews. For any other reproduction of any part of this book, however, written permission must be obtained from the publisher.

ISBN 088395-027-8

Library of Congress catalog card number: 74-79819

Manufactured in the United States of America

For my dad, who took me hunting . . . and who is still with me in every patch of cover I kick through. And for my mother, who cooked what we brought home.

Contents

1	A Quick Look at the Long-Tailed Bird	1
2	Where He Came From . . . How He Got Here	22
3	What He's Like	36
4	Where to Find Him . . . How to Hunt Him	47
5	A Few Sacrilegious Thoughts on Dogs	79
6	What to Hit Him With . . . the Ammo	90
7	What to Hit Him With . . . the Gun	114
8	How to Hit Him	147
9	Some Thoughts on Equipment	172
10	Why I Hunt	193

Hunting the
Long-tailed Bird

1

A Quick Look at the Long-Tailed Bird

November, 1946. My first pheasant hunt in four years. The previous three seasons had been spent in the Army, with the shooting—the more serious kind—coming in places like France, Belgium, Holland, Luxembourg, and Germany. Just being back to hunt in Pennsylvania under any conditions would have been enough to satisfy me, but in addition this first day afield was beautiful. Clear and bright, a bit too warm to be ideal, maybe, but even that was welcome when the memories of winter in northern Europe were so recent. A few steps to my left Chillisquaque Creek, a broad shallow stream, meandered by, ripples catching the sunlight like bits of gold, and off somewhere to my right, out of sight now, Dad was working out a patch of ringneck cover.

    I'd been moving through a narrow thicket that flanked the creek. The bank was brushy, and a tongue of high weeds extended somewhat beyond the trees, which ended at a field of winter wheat. It was a good spot to flush a pheasant. My zigzagging through the thick stuff would have moved any birds ahead and, faced with the almost complete loss of cover, they'd tend to fly. So I was particularly alert as I reached the edge of the thick stuff, the 16 gauge Sauer drilling I'd liberated in Germany balanced easily in both hands, my thumb on the safety. But nothing happened.

I'd come out on the edge of the creek, the thicket angling back to my right, nothing ahead for quite some distance except the open field and a blanket-size stand of dead weeds. For long moments I studied everything in view. Nothing moved. Yet, I felt there should have been a bird in that thicket. My gaze swept the field, the creek bank, the sky, but kept coming back to the patch of brown weeds at my feet. It was small, so small I could have spit across it, but it was too thick to see into. If there was a pheasant anywhere, he had to be in there. I stepped into it, took another step...

The weeds erupted beneath my boots. There was a brilliant flash of color, a raucous cut-cut-cut-cayouck!, and the first ringneck rooster I'd seen in years was bursting upward, his yard-long tail almost streaming through my arms. I saw the glint of a wild amber eye, a scarlet cheek patch, and tiny explosions of light where those gaudy feathers caught the sun like a handful of new-minted pennies. The rooster had been squatted at an angle toward my right shoulder, and I knew I'd have to swing completely around to shoot, for he'd be flying away almost opposite to the direction I'd been moving. Even as I whirled on my right foot I was thumbing off the safety and flipping the Sauer toward my shoulder. But when my left boot slammed down it drove into a tangle of rusty barbed wire hidden in the weeds, and my weight shifting to that foot threw me flat on my face. By now the rooster had reached the top of his vertical blastoff, tilted level, and was rapidly departing, doubtless glad to be quit of such a noisy place. Habit had kept my finger across the guard, protecting the triggers, and now as I cricked my neck to peer upward through the dusty weeds I had an interesting, if unusual, view of the rapidly disappearing bird. It would have been a simple shot had I been standing, almost identical to the high house bird from the number one skeet station. But try such a shot from flat on your belly with your cap tipped into your eyes. Things are different then.

I tried it, of course. Pheasant shooters never give up. In fact, I tried it with both barrels, shoving the Sauer out ahead of me, elbows planted firmly in the fertile Montour County soil, muzzle tilted vaguely skyward. And of course I missed. Maybe I should have had a load in the drilling's rifle barrel too, and the 6x Zeiss Zielsechs scope mounted. Then I'd have had one last chance at him as he arrowed out of sight in the distance. I cherish the memory of that big old ringneck, for as I've said, he was the first I'd seen to shoot at in years. He was also the only pheasant—or game bird of any kind—I've ever fired at from the prone position, and I cherish the memory because I missed him.

Now, looking back over the quarter-century-plus that has elapsed since that shot, years during which I've dedicatedly hunted ringnecks in areas as widely separated as New Jersey and Idaho, I've concluded that that was a more or less typical shot. Not the prone position bit. Oddball things like that don't crop up often, although when they do it's not unusual that the ringnecked pheasant should be the bird involved. Who could imagine such a situation while hunting the bobwhite quail? It simply couldn't happen. It was too undignified, too comic, and everyone knows there's nothing undignified or comic about a quail or a quail hunter.

This is what a pheasant hunter hopes for all season long—a wide open shot above low standing corn.

But overall it was typical of the ringneck. This particular bird originally had been in the thicket, and that's where you find them once the season is a few hours old. It had moved ahead of me, unseen, as I worked through the thicket, running rather than flying, until it came to the open field and creek. Then, rather than flush with me close behind, it had sneaked into the small stand of thick weeds and squatted motionless, gambling I wouldn't kick through the last few feet of cover or, if I did, that its sudden noisy takeoff would rattle me enough that it would still make its escape. And in actuality I did miss. Maybe I had a valid excuse, but so far as the bird was concerned, the result was just as he had hoped.

Maybe I'm giving the ringneck too much credit. I don't know if he actually thinks, particularly in the sense of planning what he'll do in the future, or whether his actions are instinctive. Regardless, his actions—or reactions—enable the pheasant to survive many situations which could be deadly for him. He doesn't survive them all, obviously. Millions of birds are taken by hunters each year in the United States, a majority of them, perhaps, by sportsmen of only average skill. Yet this bird often outwits a veteran hunter in a given situation.

This big kill is not difficult to explain. If you have large numbers of hunters and birds in a given area at a given time (as is normal on the opening day, when a big percentage of the year's harvest is taken), it is inevitable that many of them will come into contact. In heavily hunted areas I've even seen four lines of gunners converging on a common point in the middle of a large field—a sight to make the blood run cold when you consider the safety problem! Birds in these fields move ahead until they see or hear hunters coming from another direction. The majority squat until the last moment, then they go up in a cloud. The fusillade that follows drops a good percentage of these birds, though almost invariably there will be many more shots fired than birds dropped. Still, the birds don't have what I feel is a fair shake during such an operation. Boxing-in is efficient as a meat-getter, allowing even poor or mediocre gunners to get positive results, for such shooting is easy, but it doesn't give the bird a sporting chance. It takes unfair advantage of the ringneck's tendency to congregate in groups early in the season and gives him no real possibility of escape, although it's not uncommon for a few cold-

Birds which move ahead of hunter in fields, or those which have been knocked down but can still run, often scoot into thick cover at the field's end. Some will crouch motionless here, relying on their nerve and natural camouflage to save them, while others will continue their escape at full speed, never giving the gunner a glimpse of them.

nerved roosters to remain squatted under a fistful of weeds through the whole thing, and to escape notice or scuttle away between the feet of the anxious hunters.

This is one of the situations which makes many hunters feel the pheasant is not a top-quality gamebird. The blame really lies with these hunters, who are not top-quality sportsmen.

Ringneck shooting always seems easy to the uninitiated. They look at his gaudy feathers, which obviously should make him a conspicuous target under any circumstances. They look at his size, which is gigantic compared to a quail or dove, and still large compared with a ruffed grouse. They watch him strutting around near a farmer's barn or outbuildings—sometimes even into the backyard or, honest, up on the back porch!—and they say such a creature is too tame to hunt. They see him run a few steps off the berm of a blacktop road and, usually reluctantly, fly a short distance, often not rising above head height, and say he's too slow to be sporting.

Then you take them hunting, and they miss far more often than

A Quick Look at the Long-Tailed Bird

they hit, and some of their hits are worse than misses for they see those big birds planing down into a distant creek bottom. A dropped leg will indicate the too-far-back hit which means they'll be fox feed in the brush rather than a gourmet's delight on the dining table.

Each gunner has his own excuses for such results, and there's no point in listing them here. It would take too much space anyway. But the truth is, not until the hunter faces the fact that the ringneck is not automatically an easy target, that he is actually a unique gamebird and requires serious effort, will his kill percentage reach an acceptable level. This is not meant to suggest the pheasant is an especially difficult target. No upland bird is, if you refuse the shots which are literally impossible except by chance and thus, in fairness to the game, should not be taken. After all, the usual range is short, the pattern from your smoothbore big, so why should you miss? But the pheasant is not a grouse, he's not a quail, he's not a woodcock or a dove. All of these species are different, and the gunner who is hot stuff on one may be small potatoes on another, either because his reactions and shooting habits are grooved to a different target or because of preconceived notions which are in error.

The ringneck suffers particularly from the latter. Millions of American hunters have absorbed their opinions about gamebirds from the outdoor magazines. They might have grown up shooting ringnecks, but when they sprawl out in an easy chair at night and browse through their favorite reading material, the chances are more than good that it's a fascinating hunting tale about Ol' Ruff that keeps them turning the pages. Or, to a lesser degree, a story on Bob White. I've read such stuff myself for three and a half decades, and if I've been lucky enough to escape total brainwashing, it's due to a stubbornness traceable to my Irish-Dutch-Scotch-Polish ancestry.

Several writers have almost made careers out of writing about grouse. There's nothing much wrong with this, for a lot of what they said was true, and a lovelier bird than the grouse never took wing. However, an inevitable result of such articles and books has been the creation of a mystique which puts the grouse up on a pedestal, making him a sort of half-legendary creature which only the Abercrombie & Fitch-clad, Parker-toting gods or near-gods of the shooting world feel comfortable hunting. At the same time it was just as inevitable that the ringneck, when mentioned by such writers, would be the poor relation target, suffering by comparison each time the scribe deigned to mention him. After all, if an ordinary hunter in brush-whipped canvas pants could go out and shoot him with a beat-up, slide-action 12 gauge—or even a single-barrel Long Tom! —the ringneck obviously was beneath the notice of a real wing-shooter.

I don't agree with this. As mentioned earlier, the ringneck is a unique critter. For consistent success on him, you've got to understand his actions and, hopefully, what goes on in his head. We might call this the psychology of the bird, if that isn't too highbrow a term. We'll go into that later, but first let's consider those physical characteristics which fail to excite the uninitiated hunter: his conspicuous color and size, his alleged tameness and slowness.

That blazing color—the burnished-copper, black-edged feathers that seem to explode in sunlight; the flaming scarlet cheek patches; the iridescent purple-green-black head set off by the snow-white ring that gives him his common name, the very gaudiness that often repels a hunter weaned on the drab grouse—can be a fooler. That color which they expect will make him so conspicuous under any condition is in fact a camouflage that brings invisibility in almost any cover. As an example, many years ago Dad and I were crossing a rolling field of low clover when a cockbird came over the horizon straight at us, barely above the ground. He apparently had been flushed a long distance away and now was coming in to land, completely ignoring us. From perhaps 35 yards, when he was a few feet off the ground, I hit him. Feathers puffed, the bird collapsed in a tumble, we hurried up—and he was gone. Gone in a field of clover less than ankle high, the bird had vanished completely where there was no cover in the time it took us to trot two dozen steps. I hit him all right, the feathers were there, but that rooster had pulled the disappearing act which through the decades has brought countless curses of the ancient devils down on his tufted head. I was younger then, and I couldn't believe it. We searched long and hard in a spiral widening out from the red cap I threw down on the feathers, but we never did find that bird.

Those things happen, hunters say, they're a part of the game, unfortunate but understandable. If you take enough shots, you'll get some unaccountable results. Doubtless that's true, but it's still hard

A Quick Look at the Long-Tailed Bird

to face the fact that anything as big as a ringneck rooster can vanish like that. There's little doubt that a good dog would have brought him in quickly if we'd had one, but we didn't.

Roosters don't disappear only under catch-as-catch-can hunting conditions. Consider what must be as near to a controlled situation as you can find with these birds, a hardening pen where ringnecks are held prior to stocking. These are post-and-chicken-wire pens, fully enclosed. They come in several sizes. In my home state of Pennsylvania, the Game Commission has pens that are several hundred feet on a side and contain thousands of birds at a time. Smaller ones, 48 feet on a side, are standard for farm owners who cooperate in the raising of pheasants for release. They get day-old chicks which are placed in brooder houses until they are five days old. They then go to outside runways a few hours a day, in increasing amounts, until at about the age of two weeks they are out all day except in stormy weather. At five to six weeks they are placed in the hardening pens where they stay until about 12 weeks. Normally, 500 birds are placed in one of these enclosures. These pens contain considerable vegetation when the birds are placed there. It helps keep them from fighting, pecking, etc., but by the time they are ready for release, the area is almost bare.

At the proper time, Game Commission employees arrive to collect these pheasants, put them into crates, and distribute them to district game protectors and their deputies for release in the wild. With four or five men in a pen the "roundup" goes quickly for awhile. After most of the birds are crated, the men go through the pen in a line, only a few feet apart, moving the remaining birds ahead of them, boxing them, and repeating the process until all birds are captured.

Now, remember, this is a small pen, only 48 feet on a side, the ground inside is almost bare. There's really no place for anything as conspicuous as a brilliantly colored, fully plumaged ringneck rooster to hide. A few patches of sparse weeds and some tiny depressions the birds have scratched to dust themselves are the only possible places of concealment. Yet, a few days after these trained men have repeatedly walked their skirmish line back and forth until no more birds can be moved or seen, it is routine for the farmer to phone them to come get the rest of their birds, that a half-dozen are now strutting in lonely splendor through the dusty pen. Where did they come from? Where were they hiding? Nobody knows for certain. But they were in that small pen all that time and despite their color and their comparatively large size, they managed to make themselves invisible. Is it any wonder they can be so hard to see under thick field conditions when they don't want to be seen?

It's even harder to understand this ability to vanish when we keep in mind their size, an average ringneck rooster being perhaps ten times as heavy as a dove or quail and twice as big as a grouse. But that he disappears despite his color and bulk, there can be no doubt. It's some sort of ringneck magic, perhaps an Oriental art beyond complete understanding in this naive country!

As for their tameness, that is a sometimes thing. It's most notable during the off season, the time when most non-pheasant hunters have their experience with ringnecks. They see birds feeding near farm buildings, sitting in rows on fenceposts to dry their feathers on wet mornings, stalking through dusty roadside weeds in summer, congregating in large groups where they can find feed during bad winter weather, and in general acting almost tame. How could hunting a bird like this present any challenge, they wonder.

The answer is based on the bird himself. It's a multi-part thing, with behavioral instincts and physical attributes being important.

The ringneck is a farm country bird, a creature of agricultural regions, not a bird of the big woods like the grouse and turkey and certainly not one of the true wilderness. It has been said that the pheasant follows the plow, and this is true. In the normal course of events, this makes him a visible creature. He's not hidden away in distant hollows or on far flung mountains, he's right out there in the back forty. When not harassed, he apparently does become semi-tame, in the sense that he lives in fairly close relationship to humans, livestock, automobiles, and other ingredients of civilization. But his ancestors lived in proximity to people thousands of years, so why should he be different? They ate crops; so does he. In fact, the chances seem good that ringnecks consider those endless acres of golden corn and other goodies to be delicacies planted specifically for their benefit, something those strange-looking, tractor-riding,

Cornfields of southeastern Pennsylvania provided these birds for John Behel, Bob Bell and Wes Bower. It's often said that corn country is pheasant country and this is generally true; however, corn alone does not supply all the food requirements of these big birds.

overalled characters do as a matter of course to make life easier for the real owners of that vast region stretching from ocean to ocean across the upper third of this country. After all, what makes you think a pheasant believes the *farmer* owns that land? Consider things from the bird's viewpoint a moment and it quickly becomes obvious that pheasants aren't tame at all. They're simply living the normal life of one to the manor born, accepting what they consider their due and in their own arrogant manner putting up with oddball creatures such as you and I.

There comes a time when their "tameness" disappears—about two hours after the first gun booms on opening day. This has to be a traumatic period for the pheasant. For ten or eleven months he's had everything his own way. Oh, the weather might not have been perfect. It's often too cold or too hot or too wet or too dry to be ideal, but he got along. And there were many times when things were just great: cool mornings with enough dew to make those juicy insects easy pickings, succulent tomatoes to spear one after another as he strode down the long green row, a small grassy knoll or warm rock to provide just enough height to make him feel he was really the king when he cut loose with that raucous mating crow. Stuff like that really made a rooster believe life was worth living.

Then all of a sudden—BANG! Pandemonium breaks loose, panic erupts. Men with guns appear everywhere on what had been quiet fields, and in minutes pheasants are going all directions. Faced with a power their boldness and arrogance can't conquer, they blast skyward in bunches or streak away afoot until a sudden, unexpected meeting with another gunner flushes them. This, the opening hour or two of the season, is the time of the big kill. This is the time when the pheasant still thinks he is king of the hill. This is the time when the new hunter learns pheasants are tame and easy pickings, and if he's satisfied with his quick limit today and doesn't come back tomorrow, he can go through life believing that.

That tameness quickly disappears. The ringneck hasn't survived as a gamebird for centuries by being stupid. It's sort of traditional for hunters to take a break for a sandwich and coffee shortly after the opening flurry, maybe because everyone is too anxious to get into the field to eat a filling breakfast on opening day. Maybe it's because human nature compels hunters to compare notes after some exciting gunning, to compliment a buddy on a good shot or offer an ingenious excuse for your too-public miss. This can come while sprawled on a strip of soft grass near a fencerow or perhaps back at the car. No matter. It's just a breather, it doesn't take long. But it's long enough for any unscathed pheasants to face the fact that hunting season has arrived, and if they want to live through it, they'd better make themselves scarce. A small percentage of them may have imprinted memories of the previous season. Most of them don't, unless there's something in their genes that revives survival instincts from out of the distant past. No matter how, the remaining birds have been educated. They're not tame anymore. The new hunter in the group who recaps his Thermos, grabs his gun and eagerly sallies forth to have another wild *scheutzenfest* at the expense of these gaudy critters is in for a rude surprise. The birds have disappeared. The pheasant shooting is over for the season; the pheasant hunting has begun. Where did they go? We'll talk about that later. We still have to give some thought to their slowness and other physical attributes.

Pheasants are slow. You know that and I know it. Why shouldn't we know it, we've had it pointed out to us hundreds of times. It's hard to argue with a "fact" that goes back so far, but sometimes I do wonder about things. If a pheasant is slow, what is it slow compared

Paul Failor and Ken Hess are about ready to give up on a small patch of cover they saw a ringneck run into. Where he went is anybody's guess. Nobody saw him leave, but he just ain't there no more!

with? He had to be compared to something in the first place, or the observation never would have been made, and for consistency that something had to be another gamebird. Was that other bird the ruffed grouse? Or perhaps the bobwhite quail? It couldn't have been the woodcock. Few upland hunters ever comment upon his speed. It's only in recent years that the dove has gained widespread favor as an early-season target in ringneck country. Nor is it likely that the pinnated grouse, often called the prairie chicken, figured in this. Although common in our Midwest in the early days, this bird was driven out by agriculture before the turn of the present century. There is record of a South Dakota farmer who intended to stock ringnecks asking hunters to leave them alone because with a little protection for a few years they might drive out the "vulgar native grouse, which are not really game birds. . ." No, it seems most likely that the grouse or bobwhite aficionados are responsible for the pheasant's opprobrium. That being the case, it doesn't seem unfair for an old pheasant hunter to turn the tables and look at the speed of these other birds.

Normally it's difficult to determine the true air speeds of gamebirds, but over the years many observations have been made on most species, and some of these are highly accurate, as they were taken by radar. Whether the flights which were so well timed happened to be of birds moving as fast as they could go is debatable. However, they probably are close enough for all practical purposes.

The ruffed grouse has been timed in the open at just over 50 mph, however, his speed in typically thick cover is usually in the 20 to 25 mph class. The bobwhite quail usually flies in the 30 to 40 mph bracket, while the mourning dove cruises at about 40 and spurts to 60 mph or so. By comparison, the "slow" ringneck has been accurately timed at 48 mph in the open. Any of these birds might be capable of greater speeds, and with tailwinds they move much faster in relation to the gunner. The truth of the matter is, however, that the top speeds of the grouse, bobwhite, and ringneck are so close to identical that there's little point arguing over the difference.

Yet many hunters do argue, and there must be some reasons for the way they feel. What are they? There seem to be three basic ones: the relative sizes of these three birds, the different ways they get into flight, and the different types of cover they normally inhabit.

As mentioned, the pheasant is far bigger than the grouse or quail; not only in weight but also in size. A ringneck that measures 36 inches from beak to tail tip is about average. The longest tail feather alone often measures two feet and occasionally reaches 27 inches or so, and the overall size is twice the length of the average adult ruffed grouse and three and a half times the length of a bobwhite. If all of these move at the same speed at approximately the same distance from the viewer, obviously the largest one is going to be the easiest seen. This is particularly true when the light is such that it reflects the pheasant's gaudy plumage, making it even more conspicuous. The more clearly something is seen, the slower it seems to be moving.

They also get airborne differently. The bobwhite has to be number one in this category. From a motionless, normally invisible start, he reaches almost full speed in the blink of an eye. Where a moment before there was only the faintly quivering south end of a locked-up pointer, now there are seven brown blurs skimming over the weed field toward an overgrown fencerow. The bobwhite's tan and white coloring blends well with the typical cover in which he's found, so he can be hard to see even when more or less in the open.

And the whirr of his wings can be disconcerting, even when expected.

One of the biggest things going for the bobwhite is that a covey flush offers so many potential targets that the inexperienced hunter will often flip his gun muzzle from one bird to another to another without ever firing a shot! The urge to "get 'em all" is so strong, though obviously impossible, that it often happens none is got. Or a shot is fired at one and then a second bird is swung on though the first was not touched. In such instances the second bird is rarely dropped, nor is the third, if the scattergun holds that many shells. All in all, the bobwhite provides a special kind of thrill for most gunners, and few would want it any other way. Anyone can get a kick out of downing singles rather regularly and an occasional double makes their day, but the few cold-nerved shooting machines we've known who routinely drop two or three birds on a rise don't really seem to enjoy what they're doing. A certain degree of proficiency is always admirable, but near perfection turns most people off. But the bobwhite gets moving with such sudden speed that few gunners ever reach that level of skill, so perhaps we shouldn't be too critical. It's easy to see why many sportsmen think he's supersonic.

The ruffed grouse is, in a way, more of the same thing. "More" in the sense that he's a bigger, tougher bird, but not "more" in reference to numbers. Single birds are the rule in grouse flushes these days, although occasionally a brace will go out and on rare occasions three or four will flush. Despite the thick cover they frequent, grouse are seen fairly often on the ground—or in a tree—before they flush. Here the gunner has at least an instant's warning that something strenuous and impressive is due to occur, and sometimes several seconds pass while the grouse seems to be trying to make up his mind whether to fly or completely ignore the hunter and go on eating those frost-burned grapes. I doubt, however, if this time interval is any help to the shooter. A second seems like a month when he's waiting for Ol' Ruff to make his move, and the tension created by his surging blood pressure can wind him up so tight that nothing in this world could give him the smooth swing he needs when the explosion does take place. Maybe the whole thing is an act, a supreme bluff, the gimmick of a smart species. Whatever, the results often favor this bird too, for when he thunders into flight, seemingly zigzagging around, under or through every bit of cover on the hillside, the empty hulls on the ground far outnumber the birds in the game bag.

For many experienced hunters, or those with fast reaction times, a completely unexpected flush is easier to handle, for they just respond to the stimulus by swinging and shooting. Since that bird really isn't going very fast, despite the noise he chooses to make, a hit often results. Be all this as it may, when a grouse does flush he does it in what has been called a rather rapid manner.

The ringneck, by comparision, is a slowpoke when it comes to taking off. It pains me to write that, but it's true. Maybe it's because he doesn't really like to fly. Wildlife biologists list figures to prove that ringnecks have a low ratio of wing area to body weight. This means they have to churn out an unusually fast wingbeat to achieve their flight speed—about three per second—and maybe this is one of the reasons they often prefer running to flying. It is pure speculation when I say they don't like to fly, but anyone who has spent a week hunting these critters will accept the statement that they do like to run. At times I think this is what they do best. Others must feel this way too, for I've seen a letter to the Game Commission of a good pheasant state in which it was suggested that biologists be assigned to breed a race of "sore-footed" pheasants, the wistful hope being that this would encourage them to emulate birds more than race horses. There were times, some thirty years ago, when my beagle or basset would take off along a fencerow or through a cornfield, hot on the trail of a rambling rooster. For hundreds of yards I'd go pounding after the dog, my Remington pump at a high port-arms position, shouting encouragement to the dog and cussing the bird as long as my breath held out. Occasionally I would guess right and cut across a corner to be in the proper place, red-faced and gasping for breath, when, with a mighty clatter of wings and mouthing a string of pheasant profanity, that big old bird would finally put his faith in his feathers and take off. Maybe his legs got tired too! Sometimes it would be a hen that flushed at the end of the long trail, but far more often it would be a rooster. And, in a surprising number of cases I dropped these birds. Maybe I couldn't afford a miss after the energy I'd invested. In total, over the years, I must have chased running pheasants for miles. I don't chase them like that anymore. I couldn't

A Quick Look at the Long-Tailed Bird

if I wanted to. But they still run just as fast and far, and I can well understand how anyone who has tried to flush a runner is sure to be a great admirer of the grouse.

They don't always run that way, of course. Sometimes they don't run at all. If there's anything a ringneck can do as well as run it's squat absolutely motionless, either in cover so thick it'd repel a rhino or under a nearly leafless cornstalk where only his motionlessness, camouflage and nerve can save his skin. And time after time, they do. With a known enemy approaching (and shortly after the season opens every pheasant knows that man with a gun is his enemy, and you can believe that) a significant percentage of ringnecks will freeze rather than run or fly and let the hunter pass within feet without batting an eye or flicking a feather. I once literally stepped on a pheasant hidden in a two-foot-square clump of grass growing in the crotch of a fallen tree. It takes nerve to sit like this, but that's something of which ringnecks have a triple dose. Alongside an old rooster, a Mississippi riverboat gambler is an altar boy.

So if a rooster runs or sits today, he has a good chance of seeing tomorrow. Once he's airborne and moving, his chances are as good as those of most birds. His takeoff isn't quite as fast as the grouse's or the quail's, and a hunter who isn't rattled by the sudden appearance and sound of game can do well on ringnecks. Yet, many birds are missed or crippled on the rise.

A typical pheasant takeoff is a vertical climb which puts him above standing corn, most brush, and other ground cover. The big problem in hitting ringneck roosters flushing like this is their tail. It comprises a good percentage of the bird's overall length and, particularly when viewed from the rear on a rising bird, gives the impression it's part of the body. Biologically it is, but when it comes shooting time it's really the wrong end to hit. The gunner who uses the bird as a whole for his aiming point often misses completely because he shoots too low on a bird that is climbing at an unusually steep angle. If he does connect, his load is centered at the bird's rear end. If he waits a moment longer, until the bird reaches the top of its rise, it's a comparatively easy shot when the bird seems to hesitate an instant before gaining forward momentum. It's an easy shot on the rise, if the gun is swung up through the bird's flight path and the trigger hit as the muzzle passes through the white ring on the neck. You have to

A typical ringneck rise.

concentrate on the bird's head, not his middle. Ignore that tail completely. If you're aware of it at all, your shot will be too far back.

The pheasant, like the grouse, can also unnerve a shooter with the noise of his flush. The wings don't produce the grouse's roar but they quite often do make a lot of noise, particularly when a big rooster bulls his way up through several layers of cover. Even more disconcerting is the harsh, loud squawk—*cut-cut-cut-cuwahk*—that a rising pheasant often emits. (Hens are quieter but even more contemptuous in their own way. They tend to empty their bowels on takeoff!) The raucous blast, as with the grouse's thunder and to a lesser extent the quail's whirr of wings, freezes many hunters in place for a moment. This automatic immobility apparently is a normal reaction to a sudden danger, which is how the lower sensory levels apparently interpret the sound. It helps keep your as-yet-unidentified "enemy" from seeing you. By the time this involuntary response is overcome the bird is well on its way. Most hunters still shoot, of course, but by now they're later than they should be, and solid hits are scarcer than most of us like to admit. Occasionally on a grouse, enough pellets will get through the foliage to down a bird anyway, and this forms the basis for a "bragging" shot: "I gottim when he was completely out of sight." Or a pheasant is feathered, and this too is duly reported as if it's some fantastic feat. Actually, most such shots should never have been fired in the first place, let alone bragged about. Hunters are only human, however, and after spending hours or perhaps days slogging through rough cover trying to scrounge up a shot, it would take superhuman self-control not to pull the trigger when a bird is within possible range.

The bobwhite, grouse, and ringneck tend to inhabit basically different types of cover, and this affects shooting results too. Put simply, quail are most often hunted in scraggly farm country. The cover is essentially low, characterized by weedy fields and fencerows, sumac clumps, and similar growth. When against a camouflaging background, with their small size and good speed, they flicker in and out of focus in a way that makes you want to scrunch your eyes shut and start looking all over again. This makes accurate gun handling far from routine. When they do appear against the sky, quail are much easier to drop. Occasionally a covey will be flushed in woods, but it will rarely be far from fields.

The grouse is almost always found in thick cover, or so close to it that a short flight will put him there. He might be in a pine thicket on a mountain ridge many miles from the nearest village; in an overgrown creekbottom dividing a pair of steep, forgotten farm hills; among swampy alders or in a rocky laurel thicket. Wherever he is the going will be tough, and the shooting will be fast, perhaps impossible. This is one reason he has attracted his devoted following: he's hard to find and even harder to hit.

The ringneck, in the minds of many, is easy to find because of his normal habitat. Just go out back of the barn and shoot him. As mentioned earlier, this is possible early in the season. But I have also found—and shot at—and sometimes hit—pheasants in every kind of cover imaginable, places where no quail shooter and only the craziest grouse hunter would go. What were they doing there? Surviving, I guess. I don't know if they sought out such places deliberately or whether heavy gunning pressure in the farm country drove them there. If you can picture the densest creekbottom tangles; the steepest tree-grown, brush-and-deadfall-covered brambly hillsides you

Smart old roosters often take refuge in the thick corners found near many cornfields. Work such spots thoroughly. Over a season, they'll provide a good percentage of a hunter's shots.

ever saw; places where it takes both feet and three hands just to hang on and another for the gun, that's the kind of country I mean. Nobody ever seems to tell you that pheasants head for these places when the shooters get too concentrated (and maybe only a few of us have been crazy enough to find them there), but they are there and chasing them out and hitting them is as tough a chore as any dang-fool upland gunner wants to tackle. Of course, you don't *have* to go there . . . unless maybe it's late in the season and you really want to find some birds.

Other gamebirds sometimes are flushed outside of their normal cover too. A few paragraphs back I mentioned that grouse are *almost* always found in thick cover. There are exceptions. I killed one in Adams County, Pennsylvania, before three witnesses, when it rose from a field of hip-high weeds literally miles from anything that could be considered grouse cover. We were hunting pheasants when the grouse, an adult female, suddenly—and *quietly*—took off almost straight away from me. The gunner to my right thought it was a hen pheasant, but I saw the square tail. The shot was easy, perhaps the easiest I've ever had on a grouse. As chance would have it, two of the friends with me happened to be nationally known outdoor writers who long have worshiped at the altar of *Bonasa umbellus,* and the fact that I—an avowed *pheasant* hunter—had shot this lovely bird in the middle of a weed *field* almost brought tears to their eyes. Being scribblers in dedicated search of outdoor truths to purvey to their faithful followers, they did their best through cajolery, bribes, and outright threats to convince me, first, that this bird was not a grouse (since obviously no grouse in its right mind would be found in such a place, nor would it provide such an easy shot to a pheasant hunter!), and second, that I had not hit it in the first place. Now, I hate to say it, but this little incident does give some interesting insight into the mental workings of the outdoor writer/grouse hunter. Either category, taken alone, can consist of stalwart, truthful fellows, but obviously an individual who belongs to both bears watching. I am glad to report that, with the proof of my shot clutched stubbornly in both hands, I was able to withstand their blandishments and abuses and return home from the day's pheasant hunting with a grouse.

As usual, though, a grouse hunter had the last word. "I'm glad you at least were carrying your Model 21 Winchester," one said,

Outdoor writer Nick Sisley displays a pair of ruffed grouse and two ringnecks—a great day's bag by any standards.

"instead of that bobtailed, Browning, autoloading meat gun." Grouse hunters do have a feel for the fitness of things.

I've no intention of criticizing the grouse or any other gamebird, of course. There's not one I don't like to hunt. Each in its own way is an extremely admirable creature, well worth every hour that can be spent on it. I do feel that too many others have unfairly downgraded the pheasant. If I have any hopes at all for this writing endeavor, it's that it will help more hunters realize what an outstanding gamebird the ringneck is. I've spent more than thirty seasons hunting upland game, and I can't think of a species I don't like. At the same time, if I had to pick just one bird to chase through the remainder of my days afield, the choice would be easy. I'd take that big, bold, brassy, colorful loudmouth—the ringnecked pheasant.

2

Where He Came From and How He Got Here

They often called him "Chink" when I was a boy, those outdoor writers of pre-World War II days. Or "Chinaman" or "Chinese pheasant." And they talked of him as an "import" or an "exotic," the names gifting this now common bird with the mysterious background of a stranger from a foreign land. This talk aroused all sorts of connotations in my mind, creating vague, misty images of a world I'd never seen, a world populated by big, long-tailed, red birds that challenged faceless, Oriental hunters.

Maybe that's how it was, at least to some extent. There's no doubt about the basic Chinese background for our ringneck, and it's pleasant to retain some childhood wonders ... even earlier ones, incidentally, stemming from a pheasant my dad shot as a young man and had had mounted. It was a fine example of the species, with a beautiful long tail, yellow eyes that glared scornfully from an erect proud head, strong feet everlastingly gripping a rough bark stand—but can you imagine anyone getting a ringneck mounted today? It just shows how scarce these birds were back in the twenties, and the feelings they aroused in hunters. Maybe the hours I spent looking at that mounted bird, running my hand along its back and down the length of its truly impressive tail, made my present feelings about the ringnecks inevitable. Or maybe it was the story, which I heard often while growing up, of the doctor, moments after I was born, telling my mother, "He'll shoot more pheasants than his dad!" I never did that in a given season, while Dad was alive, for he was an excellent hunter and a fine wing shot with his short-barreled L. C. Smith. But perhaps my lifetime total is greater, as birds are far more plentiful now and I've had the opportunity to hunt them in more places and for longer periods than he ever did.

The pheasant is found, at least to some degree, in all regions of the U.S. except the Southeast or extreme Southwest, where conditions, for reasons not yet fully understood, do not favor him. However, he is not native to this country. The first truly successful planting was made in 1881 near Corvallis, Oregon, a fact which has made the Willamette Valley famous among pheasant hunters. Birds were successfully stocked in many other areas later, but this place is considered the fountainhead. Judge O. H. Denny, U.S. Consul General at Shanghai, is the man who has been given the credit for delivering this gamebird to our shores. Approximately 30 pheasants out of an unknown number of shipments actually made the long trans-Pacific journey to the farm of the judge's brother, and from this miniscule number a significant percentage of today's American ringnecks descended. This seems literally unbelievable when you consider the hundreds of millions of pheasants which have been harvested in the nine decades since, but that's how it happened. It's said there is a time and a place for everything, and apparently the Willamette Valley in 1881 was the time and the place for the ringneck, for he certainly found a home on these new shores.

There had been earlier stocking attempts. A half-century before the United States became a country, about 1730, John Montgomery, governor of the colony of New York, planted pheasants on what is now Governor's Island, and 60 years later Benjamin Franklin's son-in-law stocked some in New Jersey. These efforts were unsuccessful, for within a year or two the birds had vanished. Reasons for these failures cannot be known now. Perhaps a random combination of weather, predators, poachers, and other factors wiped them out, or it may have been disease or something completely unknown. Pheasants exist today in these same areas, though the cover is doubtless different, so it's possible that a slightly different set of circumstances two and a half centuries ago would have established one of our eastern states as the starting point for the ringneck in America. There's no use speculating on this. No one except historians can change the past, and to tell the truth I don't want to. For me, the words "New Jersey" somehow lack the golden magic of "Oregon's Willamette Valley," and since early hunters had plenty of other birds to satisfy them, there's no need to feel sorry for them now.

It seems inevitable that an American pheasant hunter should occasionally pause to wonder about the background of his favorite gamebird and where it came from, particularly because its presence here, at least in large numbers, has come about within the lifetime of men now living. Despite what the early outdoor writers said, it isn't enough to say that our ringneck is a Chinaman. The bird Judge Denny had stocked near Peterson's Butte a few miles outside of Corvallis undoubtedly was Chinese, *Phasianus colchicus torquatus,* the subspecies common to eastern and southeastern China; however, other stockings in America were made from birds whose original home was near the other end of Asia, more than 5000 miles from Shanghai. Although it is true that there are great similarities among the various pheasants found across that great land mass (some authorities state that more than 40 subspecies are native to Asia), China alone is not responsible for our bird's heredity.

Without any intention of getting involved in a scientific view of the pheasant, let's take a few minutes to discuss its background. Pheasants go back a long way, to the Miocene period anyway, which dates some 25 million to 11 million years ago. Bones from that time indicate that their early ancestors were larger than any of today's pheasants. During the Miocene these birds extended their range from Western Asia, probably the Himalayan region, into Europe, where their fossil remains have been found. These forebears died out as time passed, and the pheasants now in Europe are the result of man's importations.

Perhaps 3500 years ago, less than a drop in a bucket compared to the time span since the Miocene but nevertheless a respectable period in the history of mankind, Chinese artisans embroidered golden and silver pheasants on silk tapestries. A thousand years later the Greeks became familiar with these birds in the region between the Black and Caspian seas. Now part of the Georgian Republic of the

U.S.S.R., this district was then called Colchis. The principal river there was the Phasis, now called the Rion. During the century before the birth of Christ, the Romans gained control of much of the land surrounding the Mediterranean, as far west and north as Spain and France and eastward along the southern edge of the Black Sea. They too gained acquaintance with this bird and called it *Phasianus avis,* which translates as "the bird from the Phasis." In Italian this became *fagiano,* in French *faisan,* in German *fasan,* and in English, of course, pheasant. The Romans or feudal landowners doubtless "stocked" this bird in Europe and, later, Britain, when that island came under Roman rule during the first century A.D. This bird became one of the ancestors of today's English pheasant, often called the "blackneck."

Pheasants are gallinaceous (of the order of Gallinae), or fowl-like birds, a group which early naturalists called rasores or scratching birds. The name came from their common characteristic of digging or scratching among ground cover to obtain seeds, grubs, and other foods. This group includes a lot of species which might not appear related. There are the quail-like birds of the sub-family Perdicinae, such as blood pheasants (*Ithagenes*) and Tragopans (*Tragopan*); the Argus-like bronze-tailed peacock pheasants (*Chalcurus*), peacock pheasants (*Polyplectron*), ocellated Argus (*Rheinardius*), and the Argus pheasant (*Argusianus*) of the sub-family Argusianinae; the peafowl (*Pavo*) of the sub-family Pavoninae; and the pheasant-like birds which belong to the family Phasinidae, sub-family Phasianinae, genus *Phasianus*. These include the eared pheasants *(Crossoptilon)*, impeyans (*Lophophorus,*), Kaleege and silver pheasants (*Gennaues*), crestless firebacks (*Acomus*), crested firebacks (*Lophura*), white-tailed pheasant (*Lobiophasus*), junglefowl *(Gallus)*, Koklass pheasants *(Pucrasia)*, cheer pheasants (*Catreus*), true pheasants (*Phasianus*), long-tailed pheasants (*Syrmaticus*), and golden and amherst pheasants (*Chrysolophus*).

Until humans started redistributing pheasants around the world to please themselves, these birds were found only in Asia and some of the East Indies. The area between the Black and Caspian seas was their western limit, and a line from the northern end of the Caspian to the Aral Sea, Lake Balkash and northeastern Manchuria marked their northern limit. Small areas of Afghanistan contained pheasants, and they were found throughout India, Ceylon, Manchuria, the small countries south of the Himalayas, Burma, China, Formosa, Korea, the Malay Peninsula, Siam, Indo-China, Japan, Sumatra, Java, Borneo, and other East Indian islands. Thus they were found from about 50 degrees north latitude to 10 degrees south, over some 100 degrees of longitude, from 40 degrees to perhaps 145 degrees east, and at all altitudes from sea level to more than 16,000 feet, some blood pheasants in the Himalayas providing the last observation. Not all genera were found throughout this region, of course, and there are large areas within it where no pheasants were found. Still a large portion of the earth's surface was home to one kind of pheasant or another, even before man introduced them to many other areas.

If you like you might take the genus *Phasianus,* which includes the pheasants we hunt, and break it down into a dozen or more species and subspecies. However, there seems little point in that, as from a hunter's standpoint there is not a great deal of difference among them. Four subspecies did have considerable importance to American hunters as they were the primary stock from which, one way or another, most of our birds derived. These were *Phasianus colchicus torquatus,* the eastern Chinese ring-necked pheasant sent to Oregon by Judge Denny; *Phasianus colchicus colchicus,* the Rion Caucasian pheasant which was liberated over Western Europe and England; *Phasianus colchicus mongolicus,* the Mongolian or Kirghiz pheasant; and *Phasianus* versicolor, the green Japanese pheasant. Let's look a little closer at these four.

According to Beebe, *Phasianus colchicus colchicus* is distributed in Transcaucasia, including the basins of the Rion and Chorokh rivers and along the southeastern coast of the Black Sea, north to Sukhumkale, just south of the main east-west chain of the Caucasus Mountains; along the bases of the Kura and lower Araxes and their tributaries up to nearly 3000 feet above sea level. Their territory touched the Caspian Sea at the Kizil-Agatch Gulf. The male of this subspecies is in general a coppery red over the breast, sides, and back. Its abdomen is a blackish brown or dark chocolate, with a blue or violet gloss dominant on the black markings of the mantle and breast.

Phasianus colchicus torquatus is found in eastern and southeastern China from Canton to Hunan, north to the Lower and Middle Yangtze, upriver at least to Ichang, north to Pekin, Kalgan, and the

Ordos country. It was believed to interbreed with *Phasianus colchicus karpowi* in the north and with *Phasianus colchicus strauchi* and *Phasianus colchicus decollatus* in the west. The male *torquatus* is marked by a white collar, usually interrupted in front. Red is more restricted to the breast than with *colchicus*. Flank feathers are usually dark and rich in color, rump and lower back grayish-green.

Phasianus colchicus mongolicus is a native of the Kirghiz country of northeastern Turkestan, in the province of Semiretshensk and part of Semipalatininsk; also of the Chinese province of Kuldja including the basins of lakes Issyk-kil, Balkash, Ala-kul, and Zaisan, together with their tributaries. Eastward, in the Tian-Shan, it reaches high altitudes along the valleys of the Tekes and Kunges, tributaries to the Ili, and then throughout southern Dzungaria as far as Guchen. The male has a broad white neck ring, interrupted in front. Its mantle, chest, and breast are bronzy orange-red, showing purple-carmine in one light, green in another. Breast and flanks have a golden ground color tipped with blackish-green. Center of breast and sides of abdomen are dark green. Lesser and median wings coverts (the small upper feathers of the wing) are buffy white.

Phasianus versicolor, a native of Japan, gets its common name, the Green Pheasant, from the coloration of its breast, back, and underparts.

Female pheasants also vary somewhat in intensity of shade, but not as much as the males. The overall impression given by hens is drabness. Feathers tend toward a dull brown with black markings topside, buff below.

The first open season on pheasants in North America took place, appropriately enough, in Oregon's Willamette Valley in 1891. On opening day, 50,000 birds reportedly were taken—50,000 birds, all descended from the mere two and a half dozen pheasants stocked here but one decade earlier! This seems incredible, and it is, for that is the one word which best describes the overall effect of the ring-necked pheasant on American hunting.

The growth of the pheasant population in Oregon gave other states and provinces a source of birds to stock. They quickly took advantage. Birds from the Willamette Valley were trapped and transplanted to the state of Washington and Vancouver Island, British Columbia, in 1883, to British Columbia's Lower Fraser Valley in

The first open season for pheasants in North America took place in Oregon's Willamette Valley in 1891. Now millions of American hunters find these long-tailed birds "right behind the barn."

1890, and to Idaho in 1903. British Columbia, which protected hens from the first, had its first pheasant season in 1896, and Washington had one soon after. Idaho's first legal hunt came in 1916. To the south, in California's San Francisco Bay area, private citizens had imported and released English pheasants in the 1870s and '80s, but these stockings failed. Between 1889 and 1898, pheasants from Oregon and Hong Kong were released, apparently successfully, but their effects were blurred by multiple liberations from a state game farm which was established in 1908. Breeding stock for this farm came from Oregon and Pennsylvania.

In the Southwest, small numbers of pheasants had been stocked as early as 1872 in New Mexico and 1875 in Colorado, but these were not successful. The latter state had its first successful planting in 1885, and Utah followed about a decade later and established a game farm in 1922. Oklahoma stocked birds in 1909; Arizona 1912; New Mexico 1916; and Texas in 1939. Local conditions were of vital importance in this region, for pheasants do not prosper in the desert areas which make up a good portion of the Southwest.

The plains and prairie states provided more suitable habitat for pheasants. This is shown by one example. Prior to 1905, less than 500 birds had been stocked in our northern prairie region. Only four decades later, in the ten years between 1940 and 1950, over 82 million pheasants were harvested by hunters in the Dakotas, Nebraska, Iowa, and Minnesota. These birds resulted largely from the efforts of the various state game departments from about 1905 to 1915. They distributed eggs to farmers for hatching and released adult birds in the wild. Some state agencies, particularly in the Dakotas, Iowa, and Nebraska, trapped birds from high population areas and transported them to less fortunate regions. In Kansas between 1925 and 1940, some 18,000 birds and 100,000 eggs were distributed to cooperating farmers, while in Missouri, game farm birds and pheasant eggs were given to cooperators as the basis for stockings during the 1904–1933 period. Minnesota's first stocking efforts came in 1905, when 70 pairs of birds from Wisconsin and Illinois were released. Minnesota also established a game farm in 1915.

The first successful game farm for pheasants, incidentally, was that of Gene Simpson of Corvallis, Oregon, who raised pheasants commercially in the early 1900s. His farm was leased by the state in 1911 and became the first large-scale, state-operated game farm for these birds.

North Dakota conducted a somewhat haphazard stocking program from 1910 into the '30s. Results were poor. From 1929 through 1934, birds were trapped in South Dakota and transplanted to make the good pheasant populations of the '40s in North Dakota. South Dakota, which for some years probably provided the greatest pheasant shooting the world has ever known, never operated a game farm. Its early liberations in the 1911–1918 period were by private individuals who bought and released a few thousand birds. The high pheasant populations which resulted were based on the introduction of a few birds into habitat which suited them almost perfectly, and they just multiplied.

Stockings of Oriental, English, and European pheasants were made in the Great Lakes region. However, the Chinese pheasant either was released in the greatest numbers or had the best survival ratio, for the birds now taken in these states usually have the white neck ring, grayish-green rump, and lower back of *torquatus*.

Individual releases of pheasants were made in Ohio before the turn of the century, and the species was established in ten counties of this state by 1903. Pheasants also had been released by individuals in Wisconsin prior to 1900. In 1893 a sportsmen's club in Holland, Michigan bought a few birds and bred these up to over 200. Their first

It's the big, gaudy, raucous-voiced rooster that attracts the hunter's attention, but it's the drab, quiet hen—"the bird that laid the golden egg"—that makes pheasant hunting one of the greatest outdoor sports in America.

release, in 1895, was unsuccessful. Recorded stockings by state agencies in this region indicate that Indiana's first releases came in 1908, followed by Michigan in 1918, Ohio 1919, Illinois 1928, and Wisconsin in 1929. According to a report by Aldo Leopold, between 1900 and 1930 in Indiana, Illinois, Iowa, Ohio, Michigan, Minnesota, Missouri, and Wisconsin, an estimated 224,436 birds were stocked at a cost of $750,000, plus some 742,000 eggs were supplied to cooperators for hatching and rearing at a cost of $150,000. Pheasants were established in these states by 1930.

In the northeastern United States, the best pheasant areas are in the agricultural regions of Pennsylvania, New Jersey, and New York. This is understandable, as the pheasant is a bird that thrives in farm country. And it is logical that it should have been introduced here at an early date, for the settlers were familiar with the bird in England and Europe. However, it should be noted that the extensive farming areas now present in this region did not exist in the early 1700s, and perhaps this had something to do with the early failures.

As noted previously, the first known attempt at introducing pheasants into North America was made in New York about 1730 when Colonel John Montgomery, then governor of that colony, released "about half a dozen couple of English Pheasants" on Nutten (now Governor's) Island. These spread to what is now Long Island and a few years later Governor William Crosby asked that they be protected for a five-year period ending December 1, 1738. A penalty of ten shillings or five days in jail was to be imposed on anyone who disturbed or destroyed the birds or eggs. Even with this protection, these birds vanished. The next known stocking attempt was by Richard Bache, son-in-law of Ben Franklin, who about 1790 released an unknown number of English pheasants near Beverly, New Jersey. Ten years later an individual who owned land near Belleville, New Jersey, released more pheasants there. Nothing came of these attempts, but toward the end of that century, in 1887, pheasants were established in that state after three stockings of English birds at a game preserve near Allamuchy.

Further north, in New England, Governor Wentworth of New Hampshire in 1793 obtained several pairs of pheasants from England and released them in his woods at Wolfeborough. These vanished. A hundred years later, a New Hampshire hunter stocked pheasants,

Pheasant stocking is still carried out to some extent in the U.S., but in most areas where this bird is hunted, natural reproduction accounts for the vast majority of the harvest.

and two years after that, in 1895, the Fish and Game Commission of that state released birds. Pheasants were stocked in Massachusetts in the 1890s. Open seasons were declared in 1906 and 1907, then closed until 1914, with stocking by the state during the closed period. In Maine, five pairs of birds were released in 1897. Progeny appeared for several years, but all disappeared during a bad winter. Pheasants spread into the southern part of Maine from New Hampshire and Massachusetts, and by 1931 state stockings had been made in all coastal and some inland countries. Private individuals began stocking pheasants in Rhode Island in 1894; in 1925 the state started releasing birds.

Gardiner's Island, at the east end of Long Island, was the site of the first successful pheasant planting in New York, in 1892. A few thousand birds had been released in the lower Hudson Valley several years earlier, but these apparently did not establish themselves as breeding stock. Repeated stocking on Long island shortly after the turn of the century established the birds there. In the western part of the state, pheasants were stocked from the Pleasant Valley Fish Hatchery, on the initiative of the hatchery foreman, and from a private estate in the Genesee Valley.

Private individuals also were responsible for early stockings in Pennsylvania's Northampton and Lehigh counties in the last decade of the 19th century. Hundreds of pheasants brought from England were released here, apparently with some success, and small numbers of birds were released in other parts of the state during the next few decades. The Pennsylvania Game Commission began stocking pheasants in 1915. It is interesting to note that the first open season on ringnecks in this state, and probably the first in the Northeast, was thirteen years earlier, in 1902. In the early years in Pennsylvania, adult birds were released in the spring so they could raise their broods in the wild, then both roosters and hens were shot in the fall, as it was believed they could not winter over. The pheasant's survival instincts disproved this, and a wild-bred population increased, slowly at first, and then, when hens were protected in 1923, much more rapidly. Hens were given complete protection until 1972, when they were made legal game in the northern part of the state. Pheasants in this region are almost exclusively stocked birds. The Game Commission reasoned that once they had spent the money to hatch the hens—and the sex cannot be told before birth—they might as well raise them to about twelve weeks of age, put them out, and let the sportsmen have the opportunity to hunt them. That way at least some of the Commission's propagation expenses are recouped and the license buyers get more of a return on their investment.

New York's first hunting season came a few years after Pennsylvania's, in 1908, while New Hampshire's was in 1923 and Maine's in 1935.

In contrast with the Chinese pheasants stocked in the Northwest, many of the birds stocked in the Northeast came from England or Europe. The pheasant common to this region now is a hybrid, described in 1937 by Richard Gerstell, a wildlife biologist, thus:

"The ringneck pheasant common to Pennsylvania today is a hybrid resulting from generations of cross-breedings between the four pure line pheasants, the common, or English pheasant (*Phasianus colchicus colchicus*), the Chinese pheasant (*P. colchicus torquatus*), the Mongolian pheasant (*P. colchicus mongolicus*), and the Japanese pheasant (*P. versicolor*).

"The color and size of individual specimens vary widely. Some are noticeably 'Chinese' in appearance; others show pronounced Mongolian markings; a few evidence blackneck ancestry; while unusually light and even partial albinos are not uncommon."

The Southeast is the only region of the United States where pheasants have failed to gain a foothold. Eleven states; Alabama, Arkansas, Florida, Georgia, Louisiana, Mississippi, North Carolina, South Carolina, Tennessee, Virginia, and Kentucky, currently have no season on wild birds, though a few exist in several of these states. Nobody is certain why they don't prosper here. High temperatures seem an obvious reason, yet pheasants accommodate to the extreme heat of Southern California. High humidity is usually the next guess, but the ringneck shows no aversion to this in the Northwest. Perhaps it is the Southeast's combination of high temperature and high humidity that forms a climatic barrier. However, pheasants have been maintained by controlled breeding and stocking in Florida, and it would be difficult to go farther southeast than that and remain in the U.S., so it has been suggested that the problems of pheasants in this general region stem from their inability to breed and rear young here in the wild. This might be related to ground temperatures, for some studies have indicated that high temperatures decrease the success ratio of eggs.

Another extreme variable is soil. This is important because it relates strongly to nutrition. If the pheasant follows the plow, the plow follows fertile soil, and, overall, agricultural areas are the areas of high pheasant population. Rich soils produce plants—crops, weeds, bushes, trees, whatever—of different kinds than poor soils. Wildlife feeding on plant life in one area derives different benefits than it would in another area. In our comparatively warm Southeast, many nutrients are leached from the soil year round by rainfall and percolation of water, while in the North, by comparison, freezing temperatures slow this action during a good part of the year, and snow cover further protects the ground. In the Southwest, where snow cover usually is absent in winter, soils still remain high in mineral value because there is little rainfall to remove it.

Many northern regions underwent glaciation in prehistoric times, which brought limestone with it, and limestone supplies the calcium in the soil which is highly important to pheasants' egg production. Biologist Aldo Leopold many years ago noted that pheasants did best in glaciated areas and suspected this was due to the lime near the surface in these regions. This theory is strengthened by the fact that the prime pheasant country in southeast Pennsylvania, though never glaciated, has extensive limestone beds underlying its fertile soil; in fact, much of the soil in this region was formed from limestone. However, there are areas in the U.S. where no glaciation occurred and limestone is missing, yet, pheasants are found in good numbers, and there are areas where glaciation did occur and limestone is present but there are no pheasants, so these few comments on climate and soil are by no means conclusive answers to his presence or absence. Maybe the pheasant's lack of interest in the South is just another sign of his cantankerousness. Or maybe he just doesn't like hominy grits. . . . Nevertheless, I still wouldn't count him completely out in this great sloping stretch of gentle land. Though he's more used to the blood-numbing blizzards that howl down from the Canadian plains with scarcely a barbed-wire fence to bar their paths, it's possible—maybe even probable—that somewhere among all those pheasant species scattered across the great belly of Asia there's at least one cousin that would find just the home he's looking for in Dixie. I'd love to be alive when, and if, that day comes—just to see the looks on the faces of the bobwhite shooters the first time they turn their pipsqueak loads loose on this long-tailed tank!

3

What He's Like

The ringneck belongs to the order *Gallinae*, which makes him a shirttail cousin of the barnyard rooster, and he's a rooster in more ways than one. He's a sexually aggressive creature that's been known to stalk into a barnyard, kick the daylights out of the local bully and mate with domestic hens. Such acts are unusual, but these same aggressive characteristics lead a ringneck rooster to stake out a private territory in the spring—a "crowing" area—collect what might be called a harem, and then do his best to make certain the species does not pass from existence. In an ideal situation one rooster can service as many as fifty hens, but under normal field conditions a tenth that number is probably an average ratio. However, this does illustrate why hunting is no threat to a pheasant population. It's simply impossible to shoot cockbirds down so far that there aren't enough left to breed all available hens.

    The breeding season begins in early spring, usually about April, although cold wet weather may delay it. The sexes tend to separate during the winter months, but as spring approaches the longer periods of daylight affect the birds' hormonal glands and the sex organs mature. The males usually reach this stage in February, about a month ahead of the females. The male selects a territory and begins crowing to attract females and to warn other males that this section of countryside is spoken for. This crowing usually takes place in early morning and late afternoon, on clear calm days. It is especially noted at such times following a shower. Intruders sometimes are welcomed with violence, though usually a bold front, backed by that mysterious authority which seems to come from the knowledge that "this land is my land," is sufficient to repel an invader.

I would imagine it takes quite a bit of nerve for one rooster to even think of taking over another's territory, though the sex drive is truly an incredible force, because a crowing rooster is really an impressive sight. The rooster grabs onto the world with both feet as if someone were trying to pull it away from him forever, stretches mightily toward heaven, opens his mouth wide enough to swallow a golf ball, and lets go with a squawk that sounds like a ton of anthracite going down a chute into hell. He then follows this exhibition by beating his wings against his body like Tarzan challenging King Kong. Maybe I'm getting a bit exuberant here, but you get the idea. Pheasants ain't bashful in the spring.

After getting a hen's attention with his loud squawks, the rooster lures her closer with a low clucking sound, plays with bits of food which he sometimes offers her, and often displays his gorgeous coat in a proud strut. I've watched this with binoculars from a short distance, and it's something to see—an impressive, bold exhibition that's typical of this cocky bird. The rooster moves toward the hen, head low and neck feathers ruffled, one wing stretched downward with its feathers flared toward the female. His tail also is spread and displayed toward her. His cheek patches become enlarged and are a brilliant crimson, his ear tufts are erect. Talk about a showoff, this guy is it. He struts this way and that, switching his plumage so the most impressive colors always are toward the bride-to-be. He sometimes makes a hissing sound by expelling air. Though the hens appear unimpressed—apparently facing the fact that they can't compete with such shenanigans they assume a nonchalant coolness—the rooster usually has little trouble collecting his harem. Harem is actually an inaccurate word, for although the hens occasionally nest close together, at other times they scatter around the crowing area or even somewhat outside of it. Females apparently do not have the same territorial feelings as roosters. No force is used to keep them

What He's Like   37

within the rooster's crowing ground, and they come and go as they please.

Each hen selects a site for her nest and builds it herself. Pheasant nests are not elaborate. Some dried weeds or grasses in a slight depression in the ground are typical. Hayfields are favored nesting places, a fact which often leads to disaster during the mowing season. It's not unusual to find nests almost anywhere—along creeks, in fencerows, roadside ditches, grain fields, weed patches, or whatever. It sometimes takes awhile for a hen to get into the mood for serious egg laying. Some hens drop eggs here and there even before a nest is built, as if warming up for the job ahead. In areas of high pheasant populations others sometimes contribute toward "dump nests," nests where several hens deposit rather large numbers of eggs, again before settling down to building their own nests, laying normal clutches and hatching.

Early clutches usually contain more eggs than later ones. A dozen is about average in April, but this decreases to perhaps eight in July. Egg fertility is high, almost 100 percent in some areas and rarely under 85 percent. If the first brood is successful the hen stops nesting for the year, but because the pheasant is a ground-nesting bird, eggs often are destroyed by predators such as raccoons, opossums, skunks, snakes, and crows, or by hazards such as fire, water, and of course mowing. Hens normally re-nest and try again, and sometimes even a third time, after wildlife tragedies such as this. Their persistence helps insure the continuation of this species. There are indications that hens born to a late brood one year tend to start their own nesting late the following year.

A few days before settling down to laying, the hen progressively sheds feathers from the area on her breast which will be in contact with the eggs. This makes it easier to maintain the proper temperature, about 100° F, on them. On the average it takes about $1\frac{1}{3}$ days to lay each egg—they're about $1\frac{3}{4}$ x $1\frac{1}{4}$ inches in size and light tan to dark green in color—and after she begins setting she turns them about once each hour. Incubation takes 23 or 24 days. Some clutches hatch as early as the beginning of May, while others are as late as September, but most—70 to 75 percent—are hatched by early July. Even though the first and last eggs in a clutch may have been laid two weeks apart, all hatch within a 24-hour period as incubation for all

Pheasant nests are not elaborate—some dried weeds in a slight depression in the ground are typical. Egg fertility is high but many hazards threaten both eggs and chicks, and a significant percentage of the summer's chicks do not survive to fall.

begins at the same time. During the incubation period the hen leaves her nest for only a short period each day for food, unless severely frightened.

Pheasant chicks weigh less than an ounce and are precocial—covered with down when they leave the egg and able to run about and eat almost immediately—but for several weeks are dependent upon the hen for protection against cold and dampness and for guidance. Young chicks apparently give off little or no scent, a common way for nature to protect young wildlife from predators. When only a few days old they begin replacing their natal down with juvenile plumage—dull-colored feathers—and by two weeks of age they can fly a short distance. At about four to six weeks, post-juvenile or adult plumage begins to show, and it is complete at about five months. Male birds begin showing colored feathers at approximately two months of age; by hunting season in the fall, the average cockbird of the year is as brightly plumaged as one of 1½ years, and may be mistaken for an old bird by the hunter.

Wildlife biologists have methods of aging pheasants from shortly after incubation begins in the egg on through adulthood. The average sportsman is unconcerned about the precise age of chicks or juveniles, but he usually has some interest in knowing whether the roosters in his gamebag are, say, six or eighteen months old. If the feathers' colors are not reliable indicators, what then? The simplest key is the spur on the back of the ringneck's leg. On young roosters, even if fully colored up, the spur is a short and comparatively blunt triangle, its length from the *back* of the leg to the point being scarcely greater than the base of the triangle. On young birds the measurement from the point of the spur to the *front* of the leg, or tarsus, will almost always be less than three-quarters of an inch. On old birds the spur is usually much longer, sharper, and deadlier looking (this is a fighting weapon), its point-to-tarsus measurement sometimes exceeding an inch. Also, the spur of a young bird can be scratched or indented with a thumbnail, but an old bird's spur is too hard for this.

In cases where this aging method might be questionable and somebody really wants to know whether a ringneck was a chick during the just-past summer or the previous one, biologists say the bursa of Fabricius can provide an answer. This is a small pouch leading off the upper wall of the intestine near the anal opening. On birds of the year, bursas are one-third inch or more deep—you can probe it with a matchstick—but by their second summer or second season to the hunter, this pouch is shallow or completely gone. Personally, I never wanted to know a rooster's age badly enough to look into this.

As a general thing, older birds also weigh more than young ones. Paul Failor, a Game Commission wildlife conservation specialist, had for some years the opportunity to weigh male pheasants taken in November in southeastern Pennsylvania. His records indicate that

The pheasant supplies millions of man-days of recreation each season, as well as millions of pounds of delicious food. A chick hatched in July is large enough and smart enough to make a tough, wily target in November.

young, wild (not stocked) roosters weighed 2 lb. 10 oz. to 2 lb. 14 oz., adult wild birds having a minimum of fat weighed 3 lb. to 3 lb. 1 oz., and very large birds of 1½ to 2½ years weighed 3 lb. 5 oz. Some late releases from game farms, which carried considerable fat, weighed as much as 4 lb. He feels that small wild birds, those weighing about 2 lb. 8 oz., are often a result of second or even third nestings. (As a matter of comparison, his records also indicate that a first-year ruffed grouse weighs about 1 lb. 5 oz. when taken in the fall, with adult grouse in this region weighing 1 lb. 8 oz. to 1 lb. 12 oz. The heaviest grouse he ever weighed went 2 lb. 2 oz.) These pheasant weights agree well with the "rough" 2 lb. 12 oz. average given by Fred H. Dale for cockbirds harvested in a half dozen states as far apart as New York and Utah, and with an earlier report by Gerstell giving a 2.87-lb. average, with a maximum of 3.83 lb. and a minimum of 2 lb. for fall-killed cockbirds.

Pheasants are omnivorous eaters. The chicks concentrate on insects, a high-protein food that also supplies good amounts of water, until about two months of age. Then their taste swings toward plant matter, although it isn't at all uncommon for adult birds to stuff

What He's Like   41

themselves with insects. Grasshoppers, crickets, cutworms, beetles, millipedes, mayflies, ants, and similar size creatures—for instance, snails—are common in a pheasant's crop or gizzard. They're even known to eat mice and snakes. Everyone knows a chicken will eat almost anything, and the same can be said for this wild cousin of our barnyard fowl. Corn is traditionally the first choice on the pheasant's menu, but in itself it isn't a complete food, though many hunters believe it is, perhaps because the ringneck is often found in or near cornfields. Corn's strong point is a high concentration of vitamin A, which provides heat, but it is weak in the calcium so necessary to hens during their laying periods. Most green plants supply vitamin A, and pheasants eat large amounts of leaves and grass. They also eat wheat, barley, oats, great amounts of weed and grass seeds, particularly foxtail, skunk cabbage, soybeans, sorghums, rice, fruit, rose hips, clover, chickweed, smartweed, sunflower and millet seeds, berries, thornapple, chokecherry, snowberry, kale, sumac, dogwood, hackberry, and even cornstalks . . . among other things. Their foods vary in different parts of the country, of course.

It seems that it doesn't matter what food is available, so long as there is plenty of it. The pheasant comes closer to being a glutton than a gourmet, and this doubtless is an advantage. However, when he has to, the ringneck can get along with little food. In controlled experiments pheasants have lived almost a month without food, maintained almost normal weight for 27 days with nothing to eat but multiflora rose hips, and lived for three months in winter on greens alone. There are cases of starvation, but in the overall picture they are rare, even in the Arctic-type conditions which sometimes afflict our northern plains states. Individuals perish, but given just the barest chance the pheasant, as a species, survives. He's a tough critter.

Pheasants are not great travelers. They prefer their necessities, food and cover, close together, and if this condition exists, they may spend all of their lives within a square mile, unless shoved out by hunters, dogs, farmers' activities, or something of the sort. Even those disturbed enough to move some distance often have a tendency to return to a favored location. They are particularly static in the summer, when the living is easy, and range more in the spring and fall according to their behavior patterns and in search of food and cover. They often form flocks in winter, sometimes tending to separate

Young wild ringnecks bagged in southeastern Pennsylvania in November, such as these dropped by John Plowman, average about 2¾ lbs. Occasionally a rooster of 1½ to 2½ years will weigh 3¼ lbs. Birds of this size can be difficult to kill, as many hunters have learned from experience.

according to sex. Cold weather moves them into thick cover, and if the weather is bad enough they may forage for food only once a day instead of their normal twice.

Pheasants are largely free of disease and parasites. Some die of pullorum, coccidiosis, blackhead, eastern equine encephalomyelitis, Newcastle disease, and botulism, to name the most common diseases afflicting them, but on the whole these are not important death factors in pheasants. The pheasant's normal life in the wild protects him. He simply doesn't live under the barnyard conditions of close contact which make the spread of disease easy. Occasionally, game farm birds are raised under unsanitary conditions and infect some wild birds when released, but this is not a significant factor either.

Various internal parasites are sometimes found in pheasants: flukes, tapeworms, roundworms of various types, eyeworms, cecal worms, gapeworms, and on occasion some of these are fatal. Usually they are not present in an individual in enough numbers to cause death. External parasites like lice and mites are routinely controlled by the pheasant's regular dust baths.

Despite the pheasant's resistance to, or avoidance of disease, he doesn't have a long lifespan. It averages less than a year for roosters, less than two years for hens. Pheasants are in danger from the moment they're hatched, assuming their eggs last long enough to be hatched and assuming the hen lives to hatch them. Chicks are tasty morsels, and even adults aren't safe from the many predators that coexist in their regions. Free-running dogs, wandering housecats, various hawks, foxes, weasels, great horned owls, crows; all these and other species are known to have some effect on the pheasant population.

I don't blame a wild creature for killing and eating a pheasant or anything else it can manage, despite the fact that I put a higher value on the pheasant. A crow or a fox or an owl is just an animal that's trying to get along in an unforgiving world. I don't view his actions as good or bad, right or wrong. I am opposed to dog and cat owners permitting their pets to prowl at will through game areas, for these domesticated animals still have a natural instinct to hunt and kill, and they're very efficient at it. Again, I don't blame the animals for their actions, for they're just doing what is natural to them, but I feel it's the owners' responsibility to provide food for their pets and to control them.

Dog and cat owners have been told many times how their pets act in the wild, but many refuse to believe the facts, while others apparently don't care what happens to wildlife so long as their pets enjoy themselves. This perhaps explains why many hunters have no compunction about discouraging a wide-roaming housecat with a load of chilled sixes, an act which the sit-at-home owners howl and cry bitter tears over. But they shouldn't; they have only themselves to blame. Animal ownership carries with it the necessity of animal control, and if one person doesn't accept this responsibility someone else will take care of it.

As an example, some years back a man I knew built a summer cottage in a good small game area near his hometown. He liked to see the rabbits and pheasants in the summer, liked to hunt them in the fall. A quarter-mile up the hollow, a young couple had their home, and after awhile the mother of one of them moved in. This woman had a passion for cats, and before long some twenty or more theoretically lived with her. Actually, they came and went as they pleased, roaming the countryside like miniature tigers. Soon, what had been a small-game hotspot was almost barren of pheasants and rabbits, a situation that annoyed the man no end. Repeated pleas to the woman brought no relief. Her pets would never harm a songbird, bunny, or pheasant chick, she insisted. "All I see around here anymore is cats," the man told a friend. The friend offered a solution: the loan of his scope-sighted .218 Bee. The offer was accepted and the little M65 Winchester took up residence behind a porch door overlooking the hollow. Within a few months the 46-gr. hollow-point bullets had reduced the local cat population to near zero, and in a season or two the small game population was back to normal. I certainly don't advocate the indiscriminate shooting of cats—or anything else—but there are occasions, when everything else fails, that direct action is the only solution to a given problem.

Man's machinery doubtless causes even more pheasant deaths than his pets. Hens love to nest in hayfields, and large numbers of them are shredded by farmers' mowers. I'm sure the farmer hates this even more than the hunter, and many do everything practicable to prevent it, but nothing so far devised will completely eliminate such deaths. At a certain time in the biological proceedings, hens are extremely reluctant to leave their nests; and at a certain time of the summer, the farmer has to cut his hay. As an inevitable result, a certain number of hens die and their eggs go unhatched. One researcher estimates that almost as many hens die during nesting season as roosters during hunting season.

Countless numbers of the chicks that are hatched never reach maturity because of another machine, the automobile. The precise number killed on highways is unknown, which is probably just as well, for the waste is depressing to contemplate. That's the unfortunate part of it, of course. A pheasant killed by a car is no deader than one killed by a hunter, but the road-kill is a waste in the hunter's eyes, while the one he shoots is taken home, prepared for the table, and served as the main course in a meal that's more satisfying in all ways than anything bought in a supermarket. And insofar as animal life goes, it doesn't affect the overall total one bit. Every pheasant eaten by a hunter and his family saves the life of a chicken, a tame duck, or whatever. Even road-killed game is not a complete waste, for most of it is eaten by other forms of wildlife, an act which in turn saves the lives of other pheasants, rabbits, and similar small game which would have been killed by these same predators. And the car which kills the gamebird sometimes kills the fox that dines on it, which is something else to keep in mind.

Some pheasants starve to death each year, but not as many as a lot of hunters believe. The pheasant is a big resourceful bird and his normal range is fertile farm country. This means that food is usually available if the bird can get to it. The pheasant's powerful claws and beak let him dig through considerable snow cover to search out whatever sustenance is there. And if conditions are such that he simply can't get food, he lives off the reserves which his comparatively big body contains, reserves which smaller birds do not have. There is a limit to his survival ability, but it's not unknown for pheasants to live several weeks in far below freezing temperatures without anything at all to eat. Before this much times passes, conditions usually moderate enough to make food available.

Severe storms can be deadly to pheasants if cover cannot be found. The northern plains states are the region where this is most notable. Heavy snows combined with high velocity winds can wipe out huge numbers of birds if cover conditions force them to remain exposed to these elements. If the birds face into the wind, individuals have been known to suffocate when the driven snow granules forced their beaks so wide that the corners of the mouth split and the snow compacted in the throat. And if they face away from it, the snow drives under their feathers where body heat melts it, only to have the extreme wind and weather refreeze it into a layer of ice that destroys the insulating properties of the feathers and kills the bird.

Despite all the problems, the pheasant is here, and he's here to stay. It's a long way from China, Mongolia, and the Colchis to Oregon, the Dakotas, and Pennsylvania, but old *Phasianus colchicus* has made the jump. With maybe a hundred native-born generations behind him (And how many other Americans can boast a background like that?), he's a full-fledged Yankee now.

4

Where to Find Him and How to Hunt Him

I don't remember the first pheasant I ever shot. I remember my first grouse, first woodcock, first turkey, my first deer, first bear, first elk, even my first rabbit. But I don't remember my first pheasant, and this saddens me a bit at times. I'm sure I'd remember the first of these big birds if it weren't for my dad. It's ironic how things work out sometimes, because it was Dad's eagerness for me to get my first rooster that makes it impossible for me to remember it.

Dad grew up on a farm, learned to hunt as a boy, and hunted every year of his life. He didn't care much for paper punching or claybird shooting but was a good shot with a hunting rifle and an excellent one with a shotgun. He always liked the smoothbore more than the rifle, I think, while with me it was the reverse. At any rate, because of him I grew up with guns. He gave me a Daisy air rifle for my fourth birthday, when I couldn't even cock it, and a Crosman pellet gun when I was six, a .22 Winchester and a 20-gauge Remington slide action a few years later; he approved of my working the whole summer before I became thirteen to earn a M94 Winchester .32 Special, and he got me a M71 Winchester .348 for a high school graduation present when I was 17. In addition, he always made sure I had whatever ammo was needed to run through my guns. That was important, for I did a lot of shooting growing up. I was born in a small town on the Susquehanna. Our backyard was only a block from the riverbank, and in those days that's where kids spent all their spare time, swimming in the summer, skating in the winter, canoeing, climbing the big willow trees, building huts out of scrap lumber, reliving the escapades of Tarzan, Robin Hood, Huck Finn, and other highly admirable characters, creating fantastic roles of our own . . . and shooting. I can't remember a friend who didn't have a gun. We shot a lot, and to tell the truth, we shot most everything except each other. Cans and bottles, sparrows and starlings, an occasional flicker, and once in a great while a crow. I must have shot thousands of sparrows as a kid. Looking back, I'm not particularly proud of that, but at the time it didn't seem unusual. And from the number of sparrows still cluttering up the country, maybe I didn't shoot enough.

Anyway, when I was old enough to hunt, Dad took me. Besides the 20-gauge Remington, I had a brand new pair of canvas britches, game coat and hat, a new flannel shirt, gray wool socks with a red band round the top, and a pair of L. L. Bean's famous leather-top rubbers. Dad probably had started hunting in overalls and farm boots and I'd have been happy to do the same, but that wasn't how he wanted it. Guns I had to have, and shells, and the right outfit.

Well, I missed the first shot I ever had at a pheasant, just like a lot of other guys I've known since. It was the opening Saturday in November, chilly and damp, and we were hunting a farm belonging to a man named Billy I. Davis. We'd seen some pheasants flush from a weedy ditch leading out of the woods ahead of us. I wanted to chase them and try to raise them again, but Dad said to watch out as we got to the ditch, that there might be more birds in it. Was he ever right! A whole cloud of roosters went out of that little spot, and I was so flustered I couldn't make up my mind which one to shoot and ended up not getting off a shot. But Dad did, as well as my uncle, Jim Buckley, and Dad dropped his. Awhile later, Jim and I were moving into the edge of the woods bordering that field when a rooster blasted off just inside the cover. I can still see the white ring around his neck shining against the shadowy trees. He went up vertically, squawking, and I threw a load of sixes where he'd just passed, never touching a feather. I can remember *that* shot all right. I could hit a tomato can in the air with my .22 and once had hit a flying crow with

The man who made a hunter out of the author—
his father, R. M. Bell.

the Crosman, but I couldn't hit one of those overgrown long-tailed ringnecks. Jim killed the bird after I missed it, and I didn't have another shot that day.

The following Saturday Dad and I were moving through a clover field toward a woods, when a big ringneck took off ahead of us. I shot and the bird folded, but even as my gun settled down I sensed the boom of Dad's gun, and though he excitedly insisted that I had killed the rooster—and maybe he even believed that I did—(and in all honesty I must admit that I possibly did)—I still never felt it was truly mine. I had never come close to killing a ringneck before, but I had done quite a bit of shooting for a kid, and I had a pretty good idea where my gun was pointing when it went off. And I don't think it was pointing where it should have been.

I didn't argue with Dad. Maybe I wanted to believe I had hit the bird, maybe I agreed because it made him so happy to think I had got it . . . I don't know. If Dad had a fault it was his instinct to be kind, to give someone else the benefit of the doubt. He acted that way with strangers, so of course it was natural that he'd be even more that way with me. And so I don't remember my first pheasant, because every

Where to Find Him . . . How to Hunt Him

time I try, the image of that shot in the clover field returns, and now, almost 35 years later, I can't recall the next bird that went down when my gun boomed. It's for the best, in the end. I wouldn't have wanted Dad any different, and this way in my mind there'll always be a touch of mystery about my first ringneck. Who knows? Maybe I did hit that big old long-tailed rooster!

I remember other pheasants I killed, though, and other pheasants taken by other hunters. I'd like to describe a little of this shooting for reasons which will be obvious soon.

On the afternoon of the first day last season, Jim Bashline and I were following the rows of a field of chest-high standing corn around the contour of a low hill. Jim was slightly ahead, and a rooster went out near him, swung around toward me so that he couldn't shoot, and then crossed behind us, just clearing the corn. At 20 yards or so I dropped him with the modified barrel of my 20-gauge Winchester, and Jim's black Lab, Sam, made the retrieve. It was a routine chance, the most unusual thing about it being that Sam brought me the bird. She ("Sam" is short for Samantha) usually takes all birds to Jim; I think he trained her that way.

That was my second bird of the day. About mid-morning we'd been standing on a grassy lane that separated a small woods from a thick weed field, debating which way to go next. The weeds were soaked from rain which had started during the night, and we were soaked to the waist from going through the field and from the waist up because the rain was still going on. (I don't know why those wine-colored days all go to the grouse hunters while us pheasant bangers get the ones that should be reserved for the kooks who go for ducks; maybe somebody up there really does like them!) Anyway, while we stood there slump-shouldered, gloomily blowing raindrops off our noses and feeling others run down inside our collars, a rooster jumped skyward out of the weeds we'd passed through only a minute earlier. I don't know why he decided to go out. Maybe he was scared by a couple of other guys who were entering the field, but they were 200 yards away. He headed over us for the woods, like an underpowered, low house, station eight bird. I could tell he was wet from the way he flew and from the mist that enveloped him when my load of 7½s socked home.

Later in the week, Don Lewis, who writes the gun column for

Wildlife artist Ned Smith has just reached the end of a patch of corn without flushing a bird and glumly surveys the dense tangle beyond. He knows that if there were any roosters in the corn, they're now in the thick stuff.

Pennsylvania Game News, and I were hunting the same area. The weather was better, but in two hours we hadn't raised a bird. We finally worked around into some back fields where few hunters go, zigzagged fruitlessly through a lot of likely looking cover, and then faced the fact that we had to get into a stand of briars, sumac, and tall weeds located in the bend of a creek. It was so thick that we literally had to force our way through a half a step at a time. In cover like that you just shove your left boot ahead as far as it will go, often only a foot, bring the right boot up behind it, and shove some more. The briars tug and scrape across your arms, belly, and pants, sometimes across your face, often your ears, always your wrists. When you can't go any farther you back up six inches to relieve the tension, pull your front boot free, raise it, and tromp down on everything you can get under your sole. Then you advance a little more. It takes quite awhile to go a few yards in places like that. The dust tickles your nose, the sweat runs down all over, the scratches burn. And it can take even longer if you try to change direction once or twice just to maintain routine hunting procedure. But it's often worth it, for that's where the pheasants are after they've been hunted a few days. One was here. I heard it fighting its way up through those tangles, saw a flash of colored movement, and I missed as it leveled off at the top of the sumacs and then dipped down instead of rising at the far side of the cover. But Don didn't miss, so we had one in the bag for our morning's work—one we figured we had earned.

That afternoon we were hunting with Bob Wise on land where the pressure had been comparatively light. As we moved in line through a field of low weeds, two roosters raised some 40 yards ahead, probably put out by Bob's dog. Bob hesitated, wanting us to get the shooting. They were pretty far out for the 20-gauges we carried, but Don and I each dropped a bird. Later, as we hunted uphill through a hollow where some standing corn petered out into scrub pines backed by honeysuckle-draped trees and brush, a ringneck went out in front of Don and curved around to my left. By the time I saw it, it had passed me and was slanting back down the hollow, so low it flickered in and out of sight among the pines. But it wasn't far away, and I managed to drop it with my second barrel.

The way it curled around us made me think of a bird I'd missed years earlier. Dad and I had hunted all afternoon without a shot, and it was getting dark as we worked through a corner of woods back to the car. The landowner had taken out some old oaks, and large leaf-covered tops were scattered about. I was climbing under and through one when a rooster scuttled out at my feet, running back to my right in the gloom. Only a few feet from me, he took off, banked around in the direction I'd originally been moving, and swung around in an almost perfect three-quarter circle. It didn't take long for him to carry out this maneuver . . . not much more than the time it took me to bang three shots at him from my Browning autoloader, without touching a feather. "How could you miss an easy one like that?" Dad asked, and I didn't have any answer at all. When I reconstructed it in my mind later, I realized it had all looked so easy (He was moving so slowly!) I just stopped swinging on every shot. That's why most misses on pheasants occur.

Sometimes last minute chances pan out better. Again, Dad and I were going home without a shot. It was the tail end of the season, so we hadn't expected much, but you always hope you'll roust out something. This day we hadn't. We were cold, tired, a bit disgusted, and soaked to the skin by a drizzle that had fallen almost all day. As we came up a hill on a mud road only a couple of miles from home, I looked up to the right and saw two roosters standing in a thick, wet clover field. The rain had just stopped, and a ray of sunlight hit them. They glittered like burnished copper against the rich, green clover. Their neck rings sparkled. My mouth watered. They were a sight to delight any bird lover, and I appreciated seeing them. But I'm a hunter. "Look up there," I whispered. I was already easing the car to a stop off the road. "Get out and give 'em a try."

Dad had seen them as soon as I did. But he was thinking better. "No," he said. "If I open the door on this side, they'll be gone before I can make a move. You get out quietly and go around behind the car. If you run up on the edge of the field fast enough, you might get a shot as they take off."

I wanted him to get the shot, but even more I wanted to make sure we didn't get skunked, and I knew he was right. Holding my breath, I eased the door open, hunched out, reached behind the front seat for my Browning and sneaked around the car, quietly feeding a pair of shells into the gun. Thirty-five yards away, both roosters were watching the car, but I don't think they realized anyone was out of it. Three quick strides took me up on the low bank. The motion flushed one bird, and I dropped him. The second streaked off on foot, and I raced after him, the deep wet clover tugging at my boots, my water-soaked pants weighing a ton on each knee. By the time I reached the top of the rise, maybe 50 yards away, my heart was banging from the sudden, violent race. But, wonder of wonders, that second bird had run out there perhaps another 30 yards and stopped, looking back as if wondering what had happened to his buddy. When he saw me come huffing and puffing over the rise, he scrambled into the air just as the first one had done, and came down in a similar fashion. All these years since, I've wondered if maybe there wasn't something odd going on between those two roosters. They just seemed so devoted.

I describe these few shots because they represent typical chances on pheasants at different times of the season. You might get any kind of shot at any time, but when you look at the overall picture after many seasons, most of them seem to segregate into a few classes. The shots themselves don't vary a great deal. Most shots at any species of gamebird fall into one of only a few types, but where the birds will be found varies.

Where to Find Him . . . How to Hunt Him

Early in the season, once the first flurry of shooting at birds which don't yet realize they are targets is over, you get the somewhat routine hunting shots. You don't just go out and put up birds which might be scratching around in plain view out behind the barn, rather you hunt them in routine cover such as swales, fencerows, cornfields, and weed fields. Despite the earlier fusillades, not all of the pheasants left are shell-shocked and underground. Some are just in ordinary cover, undoubtedly cussing the shenanigans that have upset their daily routine and wondering when in blazes things are going to settle down to normal again. So you and your buddy work from one piece of cover to another, the dog ahead of you and zigzagging back and forth. If the landowner will permit you in his standing corn, you follow the rows, preferably toward an open field as that will tend to make the birds hold a bit better when they reach it, rather than flush wild or sneak off into other bits of cover. Now and then you move a few rows right or left, hoping you pick the correct spot so the smart cookie that was sneaking back alongside you will be flustered enough to take off. Generally it's an accident when you time this perfectly, but some guys seem to develop a certain sense which tells them when to cut across rows. Experience has probably built up some awareness of the time period that it takes a rooster to figure he's gone forward long enough and to decide to cut back.

When you're in standing corn, you should make it an absolute rule not to knock the stalks over. Not one single stalk! This isn't hard if you move with the rows, but you have to pick your spots for switching aisles so you won't break any off. If the reason for this isn't obvious, it's because standing corn is still unharvested and the farmer will be coming through the field soon with his picker, a machine that's designed to work on upright stalks. Don't do anything to antagonize him! Without friendly landowners, pheasant hunters are in tough shape; in fact, they aren't even hunters. I remember as a kid seeing hunters stomp down cornstalks to move birds. They hoped the noise would keep the birds moving ahead of them. Such actions cannot be tolerated today. Many landowners won't even let you in standing corn, but if they do you want to be positive it's still standing when you leave it. If you think you're too quiet moving between those tall, rustling rows and that the birds can't hear you (a thought that would make a pheasant laugh out loud if he were aware of it),

Gunner swings up on pheasant passing over him from left rear. Early in the season, when birds are plentiful, they often provide pass shooting for one man after being flushed and missed by another.

you might let the toe of your stock occasionally touch a cornstalk as you carry it muzzle up at a rather sharp angle. But this isn't necessary, even if you like refinishing gun stocks during long winter evenings.

It's not unusual to find pheasants in corn at any time of the day, although early morning and late afternoon are probably the best periods. I don't like hunting in tall corn. When it's higher than your head, particularly with the leaves draping over, you can't see anything. Even medium-high corn makes for tough shooting, for the bird normally flushes well ahead of you, and by the time he's gained enough altitude for you to see him, he's way out there. If his altitude or the light is wrong, you have a hard time telling a rooster from a hen, and then as he levels off the angle makes it look as if he's flying downhill, to be hidden by the corn. The result of all this is a long shot, and if you drop the bird and don't have a good dog, he can be difficult—or impossible—to find. Because of these factors, I rarely hunt tall corn if I'm alone or have only one partner.

If you have enough hunters to drive cornfields, that's something else. It doesn't take many for narrow strips. By zigzagging, even one driver can handle a strip that's only a few dozen rows wide, as small strips are fairly common in some regions where the farmer works alternate strips and sometimes leaves half a field standing for a week or so after he has picked the first half. The fellow who's going to stand off the drive should get out to the far end quietly and in a roundabout way. If he just parallels the corn, chances are good he'll move any birds out well ahead of him and the whole effort will be fruitless. These same rules pertain to fencerows. I've watched from a distance while several hunters tried to set up such drives without taking proper precautions, and have seen pheasants go out the far end of the row, several hundred yards from the hunters, while the men were just getting ready to enter the other end.

However, if you have enough gunners to stand off a cornfield, get them out without disturbing the birds, and have drivers to work the corn and flank it, the chances for shooting are good. Occasionally a bird will sneak out the side, but most will work ahead of the drivers on the ground until near the end of the field. Then, pinched between the standers and the pushers, they have no place to go but up. That's when the action comes. The most important thing to remember is that all shooting should be upward. You want to bag a pheasant, not your buddy.

Low corn is easier to hunt. You can drive it too, if convenient, or you can hunt it normally and get normal shooting at anything that flushes within range. Falling birds should be marked down carefully by some bit of cover, and make a habit of lining up your last view of the bird with a conspicuous object—a tree, a fencepost, whatever. Then walk—or preferably, run—in a straight line toward the object while keeping your gaze on the spot where the bird came down. If two of you are hunting together and both do this, you'll have a precise spot located, for you each see the falling bird from a different angle and the intersection of your paths has to be its impact point. If the bird is angling into high cover as it drops, it may hit a few yards from where you expect, but you have a good idea of this just from watching. A pheasant may run after being hit, but at least you'll know you're starting your search from the right place if you've marked him well.

Don't hesitate when a bird is downed. He can look dead as last December's oak leaf in the air, then take off like a goosed greyhound when he hits the ground. The closer you are to the spot where he hits, the better your chances of taking him home. If he is just crippled, he may be stunned by the fall and you may have a chance to grab him. However, this is a slim chance. It's more likely you'll see

You'll kill yourself trying to run down a crippled rooster. If you see him at short range, take his head off; at a longer distance, just shoot him.

him scooting away, in which case the best thing to do, unless you have a good retriever, is shoot him again. If you're close, you can try a head shot so you won't drive feathers through all the eating meat. If he's out there twenty-five yards or so, you can't be so pernickety. Just shoot him. Normally it isn't considered sporting to shoot a bird on the ground, but that attitude developed in reference to healthy, unharmed individuals, not broken-wing birds that are never going to fly again. The objective here is to collect the bird you've dropped and take him home and eat him. If you hesitate even a little bit in circumstances like these, some fox will enjoy your meal.

I might as well admit right here that I have, on several occasions in years long gone, shot perfectly healthy roosters on the ground. Not many. In fact, considering the chances I've had in thirty-some seasons, the temptation each one provided, and my instinct for hitting the trigger right now, I'm surprised the total is so low. I suppose it adds up to three or four out of hundreds bagged. Even this is more than most gunners—or at least most outdoor writers—admit to, but then a hell of a lot of outdoor writers aren't as honest as they could be. Without trying to make excuses, I will state that a fellow can get out of patience with pheasants. As a species they love to run, and some of these long-tailed individuals have such faith in their feet that they absolutely refuse to fly, even when they'd have an excellent chance of escaping airborne because you're so frazzled from chasing the dog that's chasing them that you couldn't get your gun to an upward angle if your life depended on it. There you are, in a tangled corner between the end of a cornfield and a railroad embankment, 500 yards from where you started to run, gasping for breath, heart hammering in your temples, sweat scalding your eyes despite the below-freezing temperature, wondering if the ankle you turned on a frozen clod is sprained or merely broken in two places. Then that damned Chinaman scuttles up the bank thirty yards away, starting another quarter-mile sprint, and before you realize what's happened your instinct takes over and the gun goes *bang* and you've ground-swiped that SOB! Do you feel regret? Maybe later, but not right now. All you can feel now is complete and utter satisfaction, something akin to blood revenge. If there ever was a critter that deserved what he got, it was that individual, particular, no-good rooster right there, that illegitimate cross between a gazelle and a feeble-minded female, that alleged bird that didn't even know what his wings were for! Friend, I've had experience with ringnecks, and I can tell you truly there are times when they're easy to hate. Which maybe is why I love 'em so much.

Consider that bird that flushed out of that rain-soaked weed field near Bashline and me. Why did he raise when he didn't have to? Nobody knows for certain. You can't read their minds and even if you could, their thought processes are probably so devious that they're beyond American understanding. We can make a guess, however, based on similar actions at other times. Jim and I had kicked through that exact area only moments before. The bird might have been moving ahead of us and then squatted when it sensed the open grassy lane ahead, not wanting to expose itself. Or it might have been huddled in that thick stuff for quite awhile, trying to keep dry. At any rate, it had to have heard or seen us as we passed, and it relied on its concealment to keep it out of trouble. But when we stopped within several yards and stood there a few minutes talking in low tones, the pressure kept building up in that rooster, much the same as in an oldtime outlaw sleeping in a haymow who wakes up to see the posse watering their horses at the nearby trough. Do they know he's there? Should he freeze or make a dash for it? This rooster made the dash, and died. This happens fairly often—enough that experienced pheasant hunters make a habit of stopping occasionally for a minute or two in particularly good patches of cover, hoping to break the nerve of a bird which otherwise will escape detection. This is not meant to suggest that all hidden birds react in this way. For all we know, most of them hang tough in there, for there's no way of knowing how many pheasants we don't see.

The birds that do flush at times like this are usually easy to hit. The hunter is motionless, which means he can hear better than if his boots are kicking through the weeds, and this often gives him a moment's warning that a bird is taking off. He's expecting to see a rooster, or at least he should be, for that's why he's out there in the first place and having a positive attitude about the situation somehow seems to improve the chances. A bird that flushes is nearby, which means he'll be in range long enough for a good shot, though trees or tall brush can complicate this. This problem is lessened by the gunner's choice of a stopping place. It's only common sense to

Thick weed fields make good cover for pheasants. They'll often crouch motionless while you pass within a few feet, but if you do put one out of such a spot he's fully exposed to your gun.

choose a spot that will permit easy body and foot movement, a place where the gun can be mounted and swung without much interference. And of course when he stops like this the hunter should have his gun in the position he prefers for getting into action quickly and easily.

With these things going for the hunter, the rooster is in a tough situation if he does take off. Still, I've seen many a bird escape from precisely such setups. Hunters are only humans, they're not computers or precisely-designed and flawlessly-lubricated machines. They make mistakes, they have mental lapses . . . they just plain miss. These facts are part of what makes it interesting. If we hit them all, it'd be so dull we'd soon give up hunting. There isn't much chance of that, though.

The incident with Don Lewis illustrates another point. After an area has been hunted hard for a few days, pheasants are hard to find. There's nothing profound about this statement. Anyone who has given it a moment's thought knows that it has to be true. To begin with, a lot of birds have been taken out of these fields, so they're gone forever. And it's perfectly logical that a hunted species, particularly one with a wild background, will do everything in its power to make itself scarce. Yet the obvious deserves discussion because many hunters do not react to it. There apparently is a common mental attitude which says that if birds were found in a given environment a week ago, they will be there today. Chances are good they would be if they had not been hunted in the intervening days, for this is the kind of cover they prefer. But if hunting pressure has been on them throughout this period, most of the birds that are left will have deserted the easy cover for the toughest places they can find. They like the thick corners—the overgrown tangles of briars and sumac, dense stands of autumn olive, edge cuttings, greenbriar-grown creekbanks. They like out-of-the-way places where they won't be disturbed, such as tiny stands of grass around a fire-blackened stump in the crease between fields of standing wheat, a spot that might not seem worth the effort it takes to reach it, assuming the landowner will let you cross his planted field in the first place. Many won't, understandably, but others don't seem to care; many of the landowner's attitudes seem determined by his personal relationship with individual hunters. Most of the time no harm is done during a walk across a given field, but if the owner has some mental reservation about a certain hunter or group of hunters, he often restricts their actions somewhat, compromising with himself for permitting them to hunt in the first place. The hunter has no choice except to observe the restrictions, but a little effort on his part can usually improve the situation.

So the hunter who wants to get the pheasants now has to go where they are and boot them out. What is a nearly impenetrable mass to a man is like a boulevard to a rooster. He can gallop full speed through an opening in the brambles that will scarcely admit the man's size 10 boot. He jigs and jitters around and among an infinity of intertwined stalks, stems, and branches as easily as we stroll through a crowd outside a theater. Here, man's comparatively large size is in some ways a disadvantage. Of course, if he were small enough to chase through those tunnels as the pheasant does, the old rooster would gobble him up, whole, for a mid-morning snack!

The hunter isn't that small, however, so he tries to overpower the stuff. He rams into it like a miniature tank, sometimes winning the battle of the brambles, sometimes losing. Hunters new to this game usually try sneaking into and through such cover, easing themselves between the various retardants. Sometimes it works, as in the autumn olive stands which are dense but usually separate and friendly growths. The same situation prevails with red maple withes, and with large leafy treetops which have been left behind in a cut-over woodlot. They look dense and difficult but actually aren't if you approach them from the trunk end and pick your way. Where you get into trouble is in the briar and bramble thickets. There's no easy way here. You just have to slam in and fight your way. Heavy canvas or leather- or Naugahyde-faced clothing is a necessity. Many—perhaps most—hunters won't go into this stuff. They'd just as soon not get any shooting. They rationalize this by saying that in the time spent bulling around in such cover they can raise other birds in the fields. And they do get out stragglers often enough to convince themselves, or at least salve their consciences for avoiding the tough going. But over the long haul they're not getting the shooting they'd have in the briars, because that's where the most ringnecks are.

Shooting is tough in here, especially if the bird happens to go out when you're all tangled up. The very nature of the cover keeps you from moving fast, and this in turn seems to keep the pheasants close. They know they're in good cover, and you don't seem to be making much progress, so a surprisingly good percentage of the time you can get shooting at birds that go out. Your gun is in fairly good shooting position at most times, because you naturally carry it muzzle up, ahead of you, sometimes in one hand by either the small of the stock or the fore-end, depending on what you need the other hand for, sometimes in both hands at high port arms. Guns take a beating in such cover, for you often use them to force your way through, spreading the briars or even swatting them out of the way. This doesn't affect the metal parts too much, but can provide some interesting designs on the woodwork. Anyone blessed with a fancy double might not care to indulge in such shenanigans. My highest grade shotgun is a M21 Winchester, which I wouldn't trade for the most expensive gun made, but I've already altered the stock so much that I don't worry about scratches or much of anything else. My primary reason for having a gun is to hunt with it, not to look at or try to impress acquaintances with, so I go where I want and the gun goes along, and if necessary I refinish the stock when the season's over.

It's harder to find a downed bird in this thick stuff than it is to hit him. Often, when one flushes, you simply back up a half-step (which takes much of the restriction off you), snap the gun up, and shoot.

The casual hunter thinks pheasants are always found in open country, where the shooting is easy, but anyone who hunts them throughout the season knows that after the first few days they are found primarily in densely grown spots where the shooting is like that familiar to grouse hunters.

Hit him twice if you have time! If you're lucky, the bird will fall outside the dense cover, and he'll be dead. If he's a runner and you have no dog, you've got a real problem, for he'll be long gone before you can get clear of the briars. Mark his fall carefully—that practice should be made an absolute habit—and keep hunting till you find him. Occasionally they hang up in the cover, never reaching the ground at all. I've seen one come down with a thunk, to remain swaying six feet off the ground, his neck wedged into the "Y" of a sumac. Having another hunter with you increases the chances of raising birds, getting shooting, and finding them, but sometimes you have to do it all yourself, so make a real effort, particularly if you knock one down. Birds deserve to be found.

If the area you're hunting at, say, the end of the opening week has not been pounded regularly, you might as well concentrate on the same kind of territory you'd hunt on opening day: fields, swales, etc. That was shown by the typical results Lewis and I had hunting with Bob Wise. The birds were in the weed fields. Even late in the same season T. R. Them, his boy, Ted, and I had similar results in the same field. There's nothing mysterious about any of this. It's just common sense. However, many hunters don't think at all about what

When a bird is down in heavy cover and you've got no dog, the only thing you can do is tramp and look . . . and look some more.

they're doing. They just drive out somewhere, load the guns, and commence hunting. It saves a lot of energy and shotless days if you do most of your hunting where the birds are.

Pheasants are rarely found in big woods area. They might be anywhere in a small woods that's surrounded by or adjacent to normal cover. On occasion they'll be a short flight into a big woods, if they were chased, but they're actually not woods birds at all. It often pays to hunt the edges of woods, as hunters and dogs working the fields will move them in, but they don't seem to feel at home among deciduous trees. Sometimes they use coniferous trees for shelter, especially if there is lots of low ground cover, and they like patches of hardwoods which have been overgrown with great green masses of honeysuckle for the same reason. When found within small woodlots, they often will be near an opening created by a large tree which has fallen, exposing a view of the sky. Normal regeneration in such places usually has produced brush or second-growth, and pheasants seem to seek these out. Or perhaps they pitch into them when choosing a landing place among the trees.

Shooting here, or among pines, is more difficult than on field-flushed birds, for the same reason that grouse shooting is difficult.

The game is in sight for a shorter time and often is concealed by intervening trees. Probably the best way to connect is with a fast swing through its flight path, ignoring the obstacles completely and hitting the trigger without conscious thought. Usually you'll get enough pellets through the cover to do the job if you just shoot automatically. If you start trying to pick a clear lane to the bird the gun will be jerking and starting, constantly trying to catch up when you see the bird and then stopping as it goes out of sight. In a couple of seconds the rooster will be gone and you'll never get a shot off, or it will be a useless one of desperation that you'd be better off saving. In cover like this you should move alertly, with the gun in position for a quick shot, and you should be expecting a shot at any moment. This doesn't mean you should be all tensed up, so tight that your muscles can't respond when the chance does come. You should be relaxed, balanced easily, watchful, and responsive to everything within range of your eyes and ears. The sound of a flushing bird is often the first indication that one is within range in thick cover. React to this; not negatively, by freezing, but positively, by immediately moving your feet to give you the best coverage of the general area the sound is coming from. If it happens that your hearing can give you a good fix on the location, you can be swinging your gun up, snapping the safety off, tracking the sound, before you've actually seen and identified the bird. With enough experience, you'll find that as you locate and identify the probable target the butt has hit your shoulder, the muzzle has passed through the bird, and your finger slaps (or doesn't slap) the trigger, depending on whether it's a rooster or a hen. Dead bird! That's the only result of a reaction and shot like this. Guys who shoot this way almost never miss. Oh, they can miss open-country, time-to-daydream shots by a country mile sometimes, but on these flush-boom birds they're incredibly efficient. There's no thinking involved. It's just a stimulus solidus reaction thing that somehow bypasses the brain. The whole point-swing-shoot doesn't take a half-second, and when it's over the bird is lying there on the ground, deader than a cupcake. The first time you see one of these guys in action you suddenly can believe in Wyatt Earp. They're deadly. You can be too.

Toward the end of the season, the shooting sometimes seems to pick up again. I don't have any statistics to prove this, but that's an

Bob Wise moves into an overgrown corner, gun ready, expecting a flush at any moment.

impression generated over the years. The seasons starts with a bang and then, in the natural course of events, tapers off as the number of birds diminishes and hunting interest lessens. After some weeks have gone by, only the dedicated pheasant hunters keep hitting the brush. For the others, having a beer and sandwich in front of the game of the week is a lot more attractive. But the decrease in gunning pressure is gradually sensed by the birds, and they slowly react to it, edging back into their favored haunts, showing themselves a bit more while feeding, and so on. I believe this accounts for the pair of roosters Dad and I saw in the clover field that day. I described only that one incident, but actually a number of similar ones have occurred, to me, to Dad, and to other hunters of our acquaintance; enough to form a basis for these remarks. Dad always seemed to be lucky on Thanksgiving Day, which comes late in Pennsylvania's season, and it was his success here that started me watching the late season results.

Pheasant hunting methods vary according to the type and size of the cover; whether you're alone or with others; if with others, the total number in the party; whether or not dogs are used, if so, what kinds; the weather; the kind of gun you're using; or perhaps even according to what kind of shotgunner you are.

In the Midwest, where I lived for some years, the fields of standing corn stretch on endlessly. A lone hunter viewing their immensity for the first time, particularly a hunter from another part of the country where the horizons are closer, can feel as insignificant as a mouse on first glimpsing an elephant. He's overpowered, awed, at a loss to know where or how to begin. Eventually he'll learn that, without help, he might as well avoid these vast stretches. The only truly effective way to hunt large cornfields is by driving, a method mentioned earlier. In the Midwest this has been honed to perfection, a quasi-military operation that often works better than the infantry or marines experience in the serious situations because pheasants don't shoot back. Here, a dozen or more hunters—sometimes there are that many on the drive alone—often cooperate. The idea is simply to get gunners blocking one end of the field, while the drivers move the birds toward them. When large numbers of men take part, it isn't safe for drivers to zigzag through the corn, so they should be fairly close to keep birds from sneaking back through, and also to make it easy to keep tabs on each other. Six or eight rows apart is about normal. No particular noise is necessary to move the birds, but it's a good idea to speak occasionally to the man on each side of you, so he knows exactly where you are. The men on the ends of the line should be somewhat ahead of the others, to keep birds from running the flanks. Usually these end men will not even be in the corn, but moving parallel to it, for the visibility is much better on the outside. These gunners should look behind them often, because smart roosters often angle out to the rear. Inner drivers sometimes are instructed not to shoot at anything; at other times they are permitted to take birds that have flushed high enough that safety is no problem. Regulations are set up by the group, and they depend on the experience of the gunners involved, the conditions of a particular drive, etc. Safety is always the uppermost consideration, and everyone should abide fully by whatever rules have been established. For a bird to get away is nothing, but for a friend to be shot would be a never-forgotten tragedy.

The standers should move into position quietly, preferably after the drivers are ready to begin moving. Pheasants have good eyesight and good hearing, so the more inconspicuous a stander can make himself, the better. It's often possible to locate yourself behind some low brush or in front of a tree in order to break your outline. If there is nothing to aid concealment, simply stand motionless until ready to fire. Don't swing your gun up if a bird flushes some distance away and heads in your direction. He almost certainly will see the movement and alter his course. Watch until he's in range, then swing and shoot just as you would normally. Pointing out birds doesn't add anything to a kill percentage; in fact, it leads to pottering and shooting behind, unless you are a disciplined gunner who thinks such shots out in detail and makes his body obey. A lot of hunters get into the habit of shooting this way at driven birds because they think it gives them more time to aim and thus will improve their chances. You shouldn't try to aim a shotgun as if it's an artillery piece. It isn't. In practice, it should be a simple extension of your body and mind, a well-designed, efficient tool by which you reach out and lower birds to the grass. We'll talk about shooting methods at length in a later chapter. For now, we'll belabor the obvious and say that the standers in a pheasant drive should position themselves so they have overlapping fields of fire when the birds come out and everyone—standers and drivers alike—should make certain he fires only at pheasants high enough that the shots are safe.

Driving involves the biggest number of gunners in pheasant hunting. It's an efficient and exciting way of hunting large areas, and it sometimes is used in weed fields as well as cornfields, though with less positive results because birds will usually flush closer to the drivers in weeds and are likely to go any direction. That is, they can't be pinched in between standers and drivers as well as they can in corn. Even if they fly toward the standers, if they flush a couple of hundred yards before reaching them, they'll be under a full head of steam when they pass, and the shooting won't be easy. All in all, this method is usually reserved for cornfields. It's used in other parts of the country besides the Midwest, but rarely with the same efficiency, perhaps because the number of men which may cooperate in hunting is comparatively limited in some states. In Pennsylvania, for instance, no more than five persons may hunt together for small game.

Pheasant hunters don't get many of the golden days the "grousophiles" are so fond of. More typical are the gloomy sodden ones that soak the weed fields and the hunters and take a certain stubborn dedication to see through to the end.

Big gangs aren't necessary for hunting pheasants. In fact, the organized aspect of this kind of hunting, the noise, the occasional frenzy—these things antagonize a lot of men for whom hunting is an escape from such business. These hunters are often loners, men who deliberately seek out the hidden corners and distant sloughs. Birds are only part of what they're hunting. There's something inside that separates them from the mass of other hunters, and they go hunting, at least in part, to escape the involvement that marks most of today's so-called civilized living. And of course there are the guys who are hunting alone today because they slept in and Jim and Bill went without them.

Regardless, the loner's techniques are different. He can't flank both sides of the fencerow, can't be both stander and driver, can't surround a briar patch while he's kicking though it, and can't make a clean sweep through a wide weed field, moving everything before him. Nevertheless, he can get his share of birds, and in the doing, because he is responsible for the results, can gain a measure of satisfaction which is different from, and perhaps superior to, that known to the cooperative hunting group.

Where to Find Him . . . How to Hunt Him

I've done a lot of my hunting alone, and I enjoy much about this method. One has an entirely different attitude about everything; from deciding when and where you're going to hunt to picking the specific bits of cover and deciding which direction and how fast to work them. You don't have to consider anyone else's likes, dislikes, abilities, or whatever. You have an independence that somehow makes you more of a hunter. Maybe this is just a mental attitude, but it's real.

As a lone hunter you naturally choose small covers. Gullies, swales, overgrown corners, short fencerows, tiny creekbottoms, small fields hip-high in weeds and dotted with jackpines or brambles. You work them in a zigzag, pausing occasionally to give a hidden rooster time to think he's been spotted, circling, moving at varying speed, rush for a short distance, then pause. You hit every thick spot, sometimes a couple of times from different directions. Before you're done with a given patch, you have kicked every clump you can find, and then, as you're leaving for the next swale, you may come back to give just one more boot to that spot which *has* to conceal a rooster. And what seems, to the uninitiated, a surprising number of times, you're rewarded with the *cak-cak-cak* of a flushing ringneck. But you're not surprised. Lone pheasant hunters who have learned their craft know that these methods, practiced in birdy places, produce birds.

Sometimes you'll see a rooster run into a small cover, and you're faced with the problem of getting him out so you can shoot. Beginners on pheasants usually try to do it the quiet way, sneaking around the edges, peering into the tangles, doing their best to spot the critter so they can somehow flush it for a shot. This isn't the way to success. A six-months-old rooster has forgotten more about the game of Sneaky Pete than any human will ever learn. He's a past master at disappearing in the slightest trace of cover; give him a thick spot as big as a dining room table and he's gone. I don't know where he goes, you don't know where he goes, but the fact is, he ain't gonna be there when you're through poking and peeking. Anyone who's hunted ringnecks more than a season can given numerous examples of his vanishing act. I'll describe only one here, as the setup was unusual.

I happened to be sitting in my car, eating a sandwich, when I saw a rooster run across a field of winter wheat and into a tiny patch of greenbriars. These briars were straight down a fairly steep sidehill from me, perhaps 60 yards distant. A pair of 7x35 binoculars lay on the car seat, so I picked them up and focused them on the briars without ever taking my gaze off the spot. I couldn't see any bird, though the cover was fairly open, making it easy to see into. While I was studying it, a hunter came out of the adjoining field, looked around a moment, then walked over and went through the briars. I fully expected the rooster to flush, but nothing happened and the man left. Curious, I took my gun and went down, expecting to find a chuck hole in the briar patch. There was none. It was spooky. I'd seen that bird run into some rather light cover that was completely surrounded by winter wheat not over an inch or so high. I'd watched through 7x35 binoculars from a short distance and never saw him again. Yet he wasn't there when two hunters investigated the cover. Where did he go? Well, I don't have much belief in the supernatural, so I didn't accept the idea that he had simply turned into a wisp of smoke and vanished. Examining the area closely, I noted a shallow furrow leading away from the briars along the bottom of the sidehill. It was only a couple of inches deep, but this, combined with the angle from which I was viewing the scene from above, doubtless was enough to conceal the rooster from my sight when he compressed his feathers tight to his body, flattened himself to the ground, and scooted away.

Most hunting areas offer far more cover than this for a ringneck to vanish into, so these birds have no trouble disappearing if given half a chance. The best way to get them out of such places is to bust right in on them, making as much commotion as possible. A bird seen running into cover usually has been scared by another hunter, so he's got humans on the mind. If you charge right into the brush, stomping, kicking, and maybe shouting, he apparently thinks you see him and quite often flushes. You probably won't know exactly where he'll take off, but he'll be close enough to hit.

There are times you can let pheasants come to you, if you know their habits and have found the right setup. On occasional afternoons many years ago, Dad would take off work a little early, I'd hurry home from high school, and we'd drive a few miles out of town to a certain thickly grown sidehill where we knew pheasants would be coming to feed. This hill was just above a blacktop road. Below the road was a deep hollow shaded by large old hemlocks. There was almost no brush in the hollow, but many pheasants lolled away their middays there because no hunting was allowed, and the whole area was surrounded by a high cyclone fence that effectively prevented anyone from sneaking in. In late afternoon, though, the birds would work out of the hollow, under the fence, and up onto the sidehill to feed. Occasionally they'd walk right into us. A short dash would drive them into the air, and most of the time a clean kill would be made on such a chance. Usually, we just hunted the hillside in a normal manner, taking shots as they came. Because of the somewhat unique setup, we got quite a few birds from a rather small area in a comparatively short time afield. I remember dropping one rooster which, when it hit the ground, flushed another. I killed that one too, but if the first had hit a foot nearer, I might have saved a shell!

I got the biggest scare of my hunting life on that hillside. Maybe I should tell you about it. It was a drizzly afternoon in late November, and I'd been playing hide and seek with a cottontail. He didn't want to run far, and apparently there were no holes in which he could go underground. I had put him out several times and had shot but missed. I was coming downhill through the rain, still halfway looking for this bedraggled bunny, when a bit of brown under a jackpine about 15 yards ahead caught my eye for some reason. It just didn't look natural there. It was about the same color as its surroundings, but didn't truly seem to belong. Then it moved slightly and I could have sworn I saw a rabbit's eye. I was tempted to shoot. I'd been chasing that darn critter all over the wet hillside, and there he sat, an easy shot. But even though that speck of brown looked like a rabbit, I wasn't sure it was a rabbit, and I'd been taught that you don't shoot anything until you're positive what it is. And so, with my gaze riveted on that suspicious brown speck, the little Remington at the ready, I eased my way down. I don't know how close I got before it moved again—more this time—and I saw that what I'd almost been convinced was a rabbit was actually my dad's left elbow in the sleeve of his old canvas hunting coat. He'd scrooched back in under the pine to try to keep dry, and all I could see was that elbow. I was so sick at the thought of what I'd almost done that I could have thrown up right there. Later, when I reconstructed the event in my mind, I realized that I hadn't even come close to really shooting. I'd never even begun to move the Remington to my shoulder. Still, the vision of the whole thing—what *might* have happened—passed through my mind in endless detail many times in the years following, and many's the time I've thanked God for giving me the sense to wait and be sure of what I was seeing before I shot. I never did tell Dad about it. I couldn't get the words out at the time, and there never seemed to be an occasion when it was appropriate to bring it up. I describe it here only because knowing about it might make someone else hesitate sometime when he's not positive just what he's looking at. The eye can be a fooler; we tend to see what we want to see, and we can make mistakes. Once you slap that trigger there's no way on earth you can call back the shot. If there's any doubt at all, it's a lot better to lose a piece of game than to shoot a person. There's always another rabbit or pheasant in your future, but consider what would have happened had I taken the shot described here.

Despite the efficiency of group hunting and the pride that comes with collecting a few birds alone, chances are the most common and the most generally satisfying method of hunting is with another friend or two. Two gunners working cooperatively can handle almost any kind of cover, three can handle it rather well. A pair can cover both sides of a fencerow, and the third man can stand it off. They can work narrow valleys the same way, while swales and gullies are made to order for this size group. Small fields are no problem, nor are average size woodlots or areas of second-growth. Though they can't cover the large cornfields as a gang does, they can take it a swath at a time if they wish. Even more important, they don't have to find or have access to the large covers that the gang requires to make it efficient. The small and medium size areas, far more numerous in most regions, are theirs. And in the end, if only a few birds are dropped during a hunt, that's still enough to make everyone a meal, whereas the big gang needs a Jeepload to do likewise.

There's a companionable feeling to this kind of hunting that's satisfying too. Quite often in today's mobile life style you get separated from a longtime hunting pal and perhaps see him only a few times during the year. Much of the enjoyment of the day comes from the occasional breaks you take to eat an apple or share a Thermos of coffee. Sprawled out in a comfortable spot, you can hear the highlights of the elk hunt he made the previous fall, or you can tell him about your double on mallards on the last float trip on the Conodoguinet. His memories become part of yours, and yours of his, and it all adds to the outdoor background that enriches both your lives and at the same time somehow contributes to an incredibly vast American hunting heritage that's never far away if anyone opens his eyes and ears. Of course, nobody thinks philosophical thoughts like that at 10:30 in the morning in pheasant country. You're just batting the breeze, having a sandwich, enjoying being there. And now the Thermos is empty, and it's time to get at it again.

In swales or gullies ringnecks tend to work uphill more than downhill. If the cover is good, they often will hold near the top if there is clear country beyond, preferring a hidden squat to exposure by flight. Angling your way up behind them, you should be prepared to shoot as soon as you're within range of the top. Flushing birds won't be in sight long, for your downhill position handicaps you. You should hustle to find any downed bird, and it isn't a bad idea to hit a falling bird again if there's time. Even a good dog doesn't find all the cripples, and at extreme range you won't get so many pellets into the bird that it's too shot up.

Given a choice, hunt with the sun behind you, or to one side. It makes seeing easier. Against the sun, it's often impossible to tell if a bird is a rooster or a hen, and in most places the latter is protected. I lost a rooster last fall when it flushed directly into a blinding sun, almost from under my feet. Don Lewis and I were working through a stand of thick grass and pines, and I was looking the wrong direction when the bird took off. It didn't squawk but I heard it flush and swung into position, the little Winchester double on its tail, but all I actually saw was a blurred shadowy figure that immediately vanished in a smear of orange-red tears. From his angle, Don wasn't bothered by the sun, and when he saw my gun on the bird he assumed I knew it was a rooster and was going to shoot. But I never would have known the sex of that critter if Don hadn't told me later.

It's always a good idea, when two or more persons are hunting together, to identify rising birds. Often the one in best position for the shot is unable for some reason to tell if it's legal game. A shout of "Hen!" or "Cockbird!" can make a vital difference. Some years ago, in a similar situation, the gunner pulled the trigger. A couple of my friends were rabbit hunting in a narrow valley where some trees had been cut off. Everything had been burned, and then brambles took over. With a pair of good beagles working, it was cottontail heaven. One fellow was in the bottom with the dogs, the other on a stump halfway up one side. The beagles had a rabbit going and the lower man shot at it, but when the upper guy turned to see what was going on, a bird was coming right at him, straight out of the sun. It was only a black shape, he said later. He assumed the first hunter had shot at a ringneck and missed, but he centered it cleanly. It thumped into the earth literally within a yard of his stump. It was a hen. Now, the world doesn't come to an end because somebody mistakenly kills a hen pheasant. In this state they were protected, however, and perhaps even more important, it was the first time in 20-some years of hunting that this fellow had ever killed an illegal gamebird, so he had ruined a personal record in which he'd taken a bit of pride. All of which again brings up the moral: Be certain of your target. And to help out your buddy, holler "Hen!" at appropriate times—loud!

  The wind also can be important in relation to pheasant hunting—and shooting. To begin with, ringnecks don't like heavy winds. They prefer the protected sides of hills or low sheltered areas when it's blowing. Kicked out during heavy wind they tend to take off into it, then often curl around to use it as an afterburner. They're not hard to hit before they gain altitude, but once they've got everything in gear and that tailwind driving them, the guy who doesn't know how to swing that muzzle might as well save his shell. In still air a scared rooster can reach about 50 mph; with a wind of that velocity added to his speed, the shooting can be more than interesting—it can be darn frustrating.

  Ringnecks don't like wet weather either. I imagine water-soaked feathers do feel sort of raunchy about dawn on a dripping day. Anyone who has seen a drenched rooster hunching on one leg under a scraggly, leaking cornstalk while the rain continues to pound down, has seen one of the world's miserable creatures.

  Pheasants are even harder than normal to flush when it's raining or the brush is wet, so this is a good time to give special attention to overhanging creekbanks, abandoned farm yards having bits of shelter around, and other solid cover. Roosters often run in drainage ditches when disturbed in fields, though, apparently preferring wet feet and a below-ground-level head to flying. They swim, too, if necessary. Sometimes I think these critters aren't birds at all, but some weird amalgam of feathers, fins, and feet.

Back in pre-WWII days, the Washingtonville area was one of the best ringneck hotspots of east-central Pennsylvania. It was close to my home, and we hunted there often. But the shooting, though great, is not what provides my outstanding memory of that area. Rain-soaked pheasants do. Dad, cousin Dave Bell, and I were driving along a back road there one morning in early fall after a night of rain. As we came around a bend, there before us, sitting in a row on consecutive fenceposts, were a dozen or so roosters, disconsolately ruffling their matted feathers and looking in general like a bunch of hung-over dandies doing their best to forget an all-night binge. Talk about misery loving company. This could've been the place the phrase was coined.

Snow often blankets the ground late in the season. This is often a help to the hunter, for it's a big aid in making birds visible. A careful study of a thick corner will reveal ringnecks which would be totally invisible within the normal ground cover. His bright feathers, particularly if the sun is shining, contrast markedly with the snow. Sometimes you can see well enough into thickets that it's unnecessary to clump through them. Snow also makes it possible to track pheasants, although this usually isn't as easy as it sounds. A solitary track often joins a few others before long, then these sometimes separate a bit later, leaving the hunter trying to decide which, if any, to follow. And it's not uncommon to find nothing more at the end of a trail than some wing marks in the snow where the bird flushed before you were close enough to see it. Once in awhile you will trail and flush and kill a rooster, and this is a different kind of thrill. Or you'll unexpectedly kick one out of a small clump of cover that has no tracks leading to it, the snow spraying upward, feathers glittering against the whiteness, his squawk an almost-solid thing in the cold clear air, and this too is an image to remember on a winter night when you're sprawled in front of the fireplace, staring into the flames, sipping a hot buttered rum, and conjuring up your favorite moments out of the past.

One important advantage to hunting in snow is the ease with which downed birds are found. A crumpled rooster can be completely invisible in the average weed field, yet he's comparatively easy to spot against the snow. And if he's a cripple, his tracks are right there for you to follow.

The kind of gun to use usually is determined by the kind of gunner you are. At least it should be. Although it might seem strange if you never thought about it, your gun and your shooting style can sometimes govern your hunting method and the particular cover you choose to hunt. Or, in the case of two or more men with different guns and different shooting techniques, it can determine who does what when working out a specific area.

Suppose you are a guy with fast reflexes, a swing-and-shoot fellow who normally centers a rooster before it reaches the top of its takeoff. Maybe you don't actually snap shoot, but your efforts are so fast you sometimes get accused of it. Your pet scattergun is a 26-inch barreled, 20-gauge double bored improved cylinder and modified, as it fits your temperament, physique, and shooting style. Your buddy, however, is not so much on the hair-trigger side. He likes to let his birds get out a ways, mounts his guns more deliberately, and swings through them with something approaching a calculated lead. He often takes his shots at 35 yards or so, instead of at the 15 or 18 where you connect. He favors a 12-gauge slide action or autoloader with 28-inch barrel. If he's an older hunter, it's probably bored full choke, if a young old-timer, modified.

With a combination like this—and this can be an absolutely deadly setup—it's only logical to divide the assignments to take advantage of your natural tendencies and equipment. Put the fast-reaction guy in the brush in the tight corners, let him mess around in there and stir things up while the other fellow waits outside at the most appropriate spot to block off departing birds. I said it was only logical to do this, yet most hunting groups don't make assignments this way. Hunters seem to believe it has to be turn and turnabout on brush-bootin'. Younger hunters apparently feeling that's the only fair way, and older ones are perhaps unwilling to let the others think they won't take their turn in the tough going; or maybe they don't want to admit to themselves that their legs aren't as strong as they used to be. The truth of the matter is, it's in such places as this that the older guy should be giving advice on the best procedure; after all, he's the one with the most experience. And strange as it may seem, the fast-shooting guys, young or old, will much prefer being in the thick spots, for that's where they get the kind of action they like. So divide the assignments in a sensible way; you'll get more birds and over a few days of shooting you'll each average about the same number.

If you're hunting alone, or if it happens that several of you are carrying guns of similar style, it makes sense to pick your cover to fit the guns. Why hunt grass fields where most birds will flush well ahead, if you are carrying a sweet sixteen Browning auto bored improved cylinder? That's an outfit for the bramble corners. And a long-barreled 12-gauge Magnum stoked with goose loads is, by the same logic, an open-country outfit. Sure, there are going to be times in any day when you'll find yourself out of your element, but you shouldn't deliberately choose to hunt such places; rather, they're just areas to get through to reach another piece of preferred cover.

5

A Few Sacrilegious Thoughts on Dogs

Dogs and pheasants don't really go together. There are quail dogs, grouse dogs, and dogs that are invaluable when hunting ducks and geese. There are rabbit dogs, coon dogs, even squirrel dogs, and dogs are often used to run bears and mountain lions. And an awful lot of them, of all varieties, run deer when you don't want them to. But I seriously doubt if there really is such an animal as a pheasant dog.

I suppose that'll hurt some feelings. A lot of hunters have dogs they use on pheasants, and they get a lot of birds with them. I know, for I've hunted with quite a few such men and their dogs, successfully, and I've owned some reasonably good dogs myself. But stop and think a minute. Would you say an English setter is really a pheasant dog? Is a pointer? A Lab, or beagle, a bassett, a spaniel? Anything? I doubt it. Sure, any or all of these species, and others, can be trained to hunt pheasants, and many of them turn in performances that range from creditable to fantastic. But basically they are not pheasant dogs, they just happen to be animals that hunt, and they can be made to adapt to this species—after a fashion. That seems to be the approach when choosing a dog for pheasants: pick something that can be "made to do the job."

There's something sad about this. Here we have a gamebird

that's distributed over much of our country, is found in good numbers, and offers many challenges to the hunter, yet we don't actually have a dog to hunt him. Maybe that's why some gunners so heartily dislike ol' *Phasianus*. The companionship of a good dog afield is truly one of the joys of life, but the canine that can work pheasants the way a good setter works quail, say, just has not been born. It's a frustration that can drive a dog owner to despair. On the opening day of pheasant season, the man who puts down a couple of pointers is just asking for problems. He knows it, he learned it last season, but hope springs eternal and all that jazz. So he tries again, and again learns that almost never does this double-be-damned, long-tailed, freakish import from a heathen country hold for a pointing pooch! He proclaims his "new" knowledge in a voice of Biblical power and anger, scattering curses lavishly and indiscriminately on both pointer and pheasant, on his buddies and on himself, swearing on the soul of his long-departed grandmother that never again will he be both stupid enough and crazy enough to try hunting this unprintable creature with one of his precious hand-honed, choke-bored dogs! He rants, he raves, he shouts, he whistles—my good God how he whistles! The tweeting and twittering that goes on in just Adams County, Pennsylvania, on P- (for Pheasant) Day would move the *Queen Mary* to the top of Mt. Everest if the energy expended on the blowing could be compressed into a cylinder and harnessed to her props. All this goes to no avail. He blames everything, *everything*—his dogs' creeping and bolting, his sore throat, his new migraine, the fact that he brought 12-gauge shells for his 20-gauge gun—on the pheasant.

And all the pheasant wanted to do was stay alive.

That's what you call quail-hunter's logic.

All this comes about because the pheasant is a runner. He won't hold for a pointing dog, at least not often enough that the gunner really has faith something is going to fly when he goes in. It's the nature of the ringneck to diddle around in front of a dog long enough to get him acting birdy, squat until he locks up, then sneak off, leaving the dog the choice of staying on an unproductive point or creeping after. This happens so consistently there seems to be something premeditated about it. It's doubtful that a good setter or pointer should be used on pheasants, unless it's to be run exclusively on these birds, for the pheasant's actions will probably confuse the dog and engender habits which you'd rather he didn't have.

Personally, I'd just as soon not hunt ringnecks with an English pointer or an English setter. It's their nature to range widely, and this is not usually desirable in pheasant country. They take off in a weed field and thirty seconds later you see them on point a quarter-mile away. By the time you get there, the bird has moved, and the next time you see the dog he's another 500 yards distant, locked up, and the whole procedure is repeated. It doesn't take many such jaunts, the weeds tugging and pulling at your legs every step of the way, your ankles turning on old furrows, to convince anyone in his right mind that this is not the way to hunt roosters. Especially since, in normal cover, you've probably run past or over more birds than the dog ever winded. The real convincer is when the dog goes on point somewhere in a 50-acre field of standing corn, and you don't have the foggiest notion where he is.

Now, none of this is the dog's fault. He's just doing what he's been bred to do. But somehow I can't figure out why anyone would pick one of these types of dog for this kind of hunting. Even if force-trained into a pheasant dog, what's been gained?

An Irish setter comes closer to being a natural pheasant dog than the English, for he tends to stay nearer to the gunner and will retrieve more readily. This species has been almost bred out of existence as a useful animal now, but one of the greatest pheasant dogs I ever saw was an Irishman. He belonged to an older friend, and he'd certainly never have qualified for any kind of a show. He was a big brute, square and powerful, so ugly you respected him on sight, with a head like a grizzly and jaws to match. He could ram brush all day, day after day, and that's where he spent much of his time, because pheasants were all he was used on and that's where his owner wanted him. The owner, an Irish cop, was even tougher than the dog, and he convinced him of the procedures to follow on these birds. What he wanted was pheasants, and he trained Mike to produce them. The results, from a shooter's standpoint, were impressive. Mike pointed when the occasion permitted (if you can picture a Sherman tank pointing), flushed occasional birds (but usually within range), and brought back anything that came down. And after the season was a few days old, he brought back a lot of pheasants that his owner never

German shorthair eases up on a squatted bird, as hunter waits expectantly.

dropped—broken winged birds that other hunters hadn't found. Sometimes the floor of the car trunk was covered when they went home and maybe a shot hadn't been fired. There was nothing too fancy or soul-satisfying about most of this, but it was gosh-awful efficient.

Another friend had a German shorthair that was good on ringnecks. He'd get out there at times, but usually not as far as an English pointer, and most of the time he'd be happy working fairly close. He also retrieved willingly, and that's a help to a hunter.

The retrievers and spaniels that I've had experience with always seemed better pheasants dogs to me than the English pointer and setter. They find game, flush it, and if you hit it they bring it back.

I know the idea of using a retriever as a flushing dog is enough to give some traditional hunters the screaming vapors, but that's how many of them are being worked now, particularly the Labs, and they do an excellent job. The purists still believe retrievers should stay close behind or alongside the hunter and venture out only to bring back downed game; some insist these dogs should not even be used in upland covers but be restricted to waterfowl use. These feelings

Sylvia Bashline reaches for ringneck being returned by Sam (short for Samantha), a great retriever who would rather hunt than do anything else she's ever tried. A good retrieving dog takes much of the worry out of downing pheasants in thick cover or at long range. Labs, in the opinion of many ringneck hunters, are the best breed for this big bird.

are being swept aside by the American gunner's pragmatic approach; he's learned that a Lab, say, can easily be trained to work close to the hunter, that he has a good nose which helps him find and flush game, and that when it's down it has a slim chance of remaining unfound and undelivered. A few decades ago a Lab was a rarity in pheasant covers; now he's so common that he doesn't rate an inquisitive glance. His performance has been the convincer. Pheasant hunters haven't yet reached the realm of abstract theory which places so much emphasis on esoteric niceties; they just want results. That's what a good Lab gives them.

The Lab has both the physical and mental equipment to deal with a gamebird of the pheasant's size. He's easily trained, anxious to please, and his short hair makes him easy to care for after a day in thick cover. I admit to a fondness for this breed, but my feeling is based on field observation. He does the job. He continues to do it when waterfowl season comes in too, which can be a plus in a hunter's assessment.

The spaniels have always been expected to work in front of the gun, flush and retrieve birds. Before WWII I had a cocker that was a joy to hunt with. Cockers were hunting dogs in those days, some of them anyway, and Buzz certainly enjoyed it. I don't know if she was really good or just seemed that way to me (I was younger then.), but we sure had a lot of fun. Her nose went into every bit of cover within 25 yards of the gun, stub tail vibrating, eyes glistening, and when a bird went out you'd have thought it was Christmas and the Fourth of July rolled up in one! She was really too small to retrieve a big rooster, but she did it anyway, stepping all over herself and the bird as she brought it in. I don't know if there are any hunting cockers left, and somehow I can't picture them working the jungles I hunt so often now, but it's nice to remember Buzz. She died while I was in Europe during the war.

The English springer spaniel is sort of more of the same thing, big enough to do easily what can be a real chore for a cocker. I could be happy with a springer in pheasant country.

The Brittany is gaining converts every year, and deservedly so. This is the only spaniel that regularly points, he prefers to work close—unless you unfortunately get one of those developed for field trials—and he's just generally nice to be around. Several that I've hunted with have taught themselves to circle in front of running roosters and hold the baffled bird for the hunter. This is a highly admirable trait in a pheasant dog.

Hounds aren't usually thought of as pheasant dogs, but as I said earlier, no dog is really thought of as a pheasant dog, so we might as well mention at least one hound here, the beagle. From a shooting man's standpoint, you can't avoid this breed, because if getting birds is your basic objective you could well settle on a beagle. Most of them are not great on birds, but occasionally, either through temperament or training, one is outstanding.

I've killed a lot of birds put out by beagles because they were about all we had in the dog line when I was growing up. The best I ever hunted with is Paul Failor's little female, Penny. Penny has a feeling for pheasants, a fine nose, determination, courage, all the attributes you want in a hunting dog. And she's small—tiny would be a better word—maybe 11 inches at the shoulder and 11 pounds, with narrow shoulders that make it easy for her to maneuver under and through almost any cover that a pheasant can penetrate. Penny is made to order for the small, briar-grown gulleys and thickets, the brushy creekbanks, the overgrown and abandoned farm dumps where the smart old roosters love to hide. When she squirms into one of these messes and a couple of hunters cover the perimeter, action is pretty well assured. And most of the time Penny will retrieve downed birds, or at least bring them back far enough for you to see. Considering that a rooster looks bigger than she does, even though he doesn't weigh as much, this seems a reasonable compromise to me. Most beagles don't retrieve at all, and a lot of them don't perform well on any birds, but it's quite possible to get a humdinger if you make the effort and encourage it a bit.

There are other useful dogs too. Nobody ever seems to mention that fact in print, but many mongrel farm dogs are proficient at finding and flushing birds, simply because they are hunters by nature and have a lot of opportunity to practice. I guess it's beneath the dignity of some people to hunt with, or even admit the existence of, mixed-breed dogs, but some of the most productive and enjoyable days I've ever had afield were behind such four-footed fellows. Bob Wise, a hunting friend, has one that's an outstanding example. I've no idea of its ancestry. It's a long-haired dog, black, bigger than small

It's often just swing and shoot . . . and a bird falling out of the air.
Joe Osman took these pictures.

Paul Failor, a friend of many years who died while this book was in preparation, and his beagle Penny. This little dog loves to squeeze into and under the thickest cover—places few critters but an old ringneck will go—and if a bird is in there, she puts him out.

but not much, with a face something like fox. Most hunters wouldn't even look at it long enough to decide it was unimpressive, but when it comes to finding roosters, this dog has it. In less than an hour one afternoon last season, three of us limited out hunting with it, and the dog flushed and found every bird, including one broken-wing cripple. The first shooting came in a medium-height grass field, then we got a few birds out of a shallow valley split by a narrow creek and overgrown with high grass, cattails, brambles, etc., and then we found a couple more in a sumac-covered corner. Such places are not ideal for exhibiting fancy dog work because most of the time you can't even see the dog. Here's where the birds are, however, and here's where a dog like this one pays for its keep. There was nothing unusual about that afternoon's hunting. I've hunted with Bob and his dog a number of times, and though we don't always get out birds so quickly, we usually get them.

A few times a season I hunt with another friend who owns a large dairy farm. He could have any dog or dogs he might want, but all he has is a pack of mixed-blood farm dogs of all sizes and descriptions. It's some experience to go through a field behind that motley collection, I'll tell you! When they make a swath through the greenery, anything in there goes out, and at times the action is fast and furious.

Just the suggestion of such shenanigans is enough to give a blue-blooded quail hunter apoplexy, I know. Bobwhite hunters are blessed with a bird that will allow a good dog to show all his innate ability, finesse, and training, and to some sportsmen this has become the ultimate goal. They don't really go afield to shoot birds any more, but rather to watch and enjoy the performance of their dogs. The idea of a pack of mongrels simply rousting out birds for someone to shoot is an indelicate act that offends their sensibilities. Quail hunters passed that stage generations ago. Now they avoid all the crudities of hunting and exist—or give the impression that they exist—on a plane that's almost ethereal. There's nothing wrong with that, I guess, and it's possible that pheasant hunters will achieve a similar plateau some day. Personally, I'd just as soon miss it, because to me it's too much like not hunting at all!

6

What to Hit Him With —the Ammo

Pheasants are not indestructible. They just seem that way at times. Consider a rooster I shot a couple of seasons back. I was standing near a corner of woods where it jutted into a field, waiting for a buddy to work up to me, when this bird rose out of the weeds just to my left. Apparently this was another case where a prolonged pause broke a pheasant's nerve. I automatically swung the Browning autoloader and touched off a heavy load of 6s. The bird went down with a thud. I remember thinking I should have waited until it was out farther, for it wasn't more than a dozen steps from me, perfectly broadside, when I shot. I felt sure this ringneck was hit hard, but when I picked it up it wasn't dead. I chopped the back of its head with the edge of my hand, felt the bird stiffen, and slid it into my game vest. Awhile later I felt it moving about. I've known of pheasants that actually escaped from a hunter's coat and made their getaway, but this one didn't, because I now took time to make certain it was dead.

When I cleaned that bird, I found I'd centered it in my pattern. There was scarcely a square inch of the side of its body toward me that didn't have a pellet hole in it, and the shot had been taken at close range where the load's energy was high. Still, I hadn't got an immediate kill. Possibly the bird's wings were down when the load arrived, making it necessary for the shot to penetrate the near one before entering the body, which would have slowed it down somewhat. There's no way for me to know now. Nevertheless, that rooster absorbed an overpowering amount of kinetic energy without succumbing. This sort of thing happens often enough with pheasants—though it isn't actually a typical result—to make most experienced gunners definitely favor heavy loads for them.

It's possible that had I been shooting smaller shot, such as 7½s instead of 6s, I might have gotten an instant kill, for the denser pattern might have put a pellet into the brain or nearby spinal column. Heavier shot, even if fewer hit, might by chance have given better placement—and undoubtedly better penetration—which could have resulted in an immediate kill. These are the things of which you can never be certain. Each shot is unique, even if range and angle happen to be the same, for no two shot patterns are identical even if they deliver the same number of pellets on a given size target. Each is a genuinely random thing and thus places those pellets at different places. When the target is a gamebird, a quarter-inch variation in placement can be the difference between an instant kill and a cripple—perhaps a cripple that escapes. All we can do is base our expectations on past experience.

With the foregoing in mind, the question arises: what does it take to cleanly kill a given gamebird? Opinions vary somewhat, but still there is general agreement among numerous experts. Jack O'Connor writes that it takes four or five pellets of the proper size striking the bird's body, and specifies No. 4 for mallards, No. 6 for pheasants, and No. 7½ or No. 8 for quail. He doesn't directly discuss pellet energy, but implies that at any range where a pattern will give this density on the bird being hunted, energy will be adequate. Francis Sell says that multiple hits are necessary for consistent results, with five pellets each having not less than 3 foot pounds (fp) of energy needed for geese, to four hits with individual pellet energy fo 2 fp for ducks, or six to eight with 1¼ to 1½ fp. Major Burrard gives a bit more complicated frame of reference. He weighed many dead gamebirds, measured the areas of their bodies as viewed from below with feathers removed, assumed that half of this area was the truly vital part, and concluded that reasonable minimum numbers for hits

For close-flushing pheasants, 1¼ oz. of 7½ shot provides a dense, killing pattern, even from an open-bored gun.

in this area required to ensure clean kills were two for birds under 1 lb., three for birds over 1 lb., and possibly four for large strong birds such as geese. His observations were based on the use of British No. 6 shot, which is somewhat smaller than American No. 6, having an average 270 pellets per ounce compared with 225 for ours. (It would be about No. 6½ by our measuring system.) He also assumed that in all cases penetration would be acceptable.

Burrard's assumption that only half the area presented to the shot by a gamebird's body is truly vital seems logical to me. A pheasant with one or two No. 6 shot through the entrails is definitely seriously wounded, as is a deer with a .30-caliber bullet through the paunch. In both cases, the wounds will probably cause death. But many times, especially in the case of the bird which cannot be trailed, the creature will not be found by the man who shot him and will be wasted.

After weighing and measuring many gamebirds, Major Burrard noted there was a consistent ratio between weights of various species and their areas as viewed by the gunner from below (which is not greatly different from a side view). For English ringnecks, which aren't significantly different from our birds in profile, the area in square inches equaled 86% of the bird's weight in ounces. Thus a 3 lb. (48 oz.) ringneck has a body area of 41 square inches, a 2½ lb. bird (40 oz.) 34½ sq. in., and a 2 lb. bird (32 oz.) 27½ square inches. If we accept Burrard's thesis, and since we know the number of shot in a given charge, the energy of individual pellets at specified ranges, and the pattern density, which is a percentage of the shot charge that strikes within a 30-inch circle at 40 yards, we can closely calculate the effectiveness of any load.

For instance, suppose we are shooting 12-gauge shells using 1¼ oz. of No. 6 shot with a muzzle velocity of 1330 feet per second and our gun throws full choke patterns averaging 70%. The shot charge contains 281 pellets, which means we'll have 197 of them in a 30-inch circle at 40 yards. This circle contains about 707 square inches, so our density will be about one pellet for each 3.6 square inches. A 2½-pound rooster has 34½ square inches of body area, or 17-plus inches of vital area per Burrard, which means we'll average almost five pellets in this region. At 40 yards, each No. 6 pellet in this load has 2½ foot pounds of energy, so its deadliness at this distance is obvious. If we were shooting the same load in a gun giving improved cylinder or 50% patterns, we'd average one pellet per five square inches or three to four in the vital region, which also would be sufficient. With 1½ oz. of No. 2s (113 pellets), a 70% pattern would give 79 pellets in the 30-inch circle or one for every 9 square inches, which would put two in the vital area, while a 50% pattern would give 57 pellets—one per each 12½ square inches—or probably only one in the killing region. At 40 yards a No. 2 pellet started at 1330 fs has almost 8 fp of energy left, so two pellets would doubtless kill and one probably would. However, the greatly reduced number of No. 2s in this load, compared with No. 6s, increases the possibility of a random dispersion putting no pellets in the killing area. With the 6s, even if chance cuts down on the number of pellets connecting properly, the excess pellets will still do the job. If the single No. 2 from the improved cylinder choke misses, you're out of luck.

As larger shot pellets retain velocity and energy better than small ones, we can try to increase their normal pattern densities by using heavier shot charges. However, there are practical limits to the total weight that can be utilized. A given shell case has only so much volume available for shot, acceptable recoil and other factors must be considered. Going to a larger gauge provides more capacity, but the increased gun size and weight is cumbersome and slows the gunner down, sometimes so much that little practical gain is made, for by the time a shot is gotten off the bird has moved far enough away that the pattern density is back where it was when we started.

Recognizing that absolute answers are impossible, it's still natural for a new hunter to ask, "What's the best load for pheasants?" That's a question I like to hear, for it means everybody present who's ever shot one of these birds is going to throw in his two cents worth. Who knows, somewhere along the line somebody might come up with an answer that'll defy contradiction. I doubt it, though I'll give it a try myself, later on. Most of them stuff their guns full (or as full as the law allows; in repeaters this is usually two shells in the magazine and a third in the chamber) of what is colloquially called "high base" shells* carrying at least 1¼ oz. of No. 6 shot.

They use this combination because it works. It works in the tiny fields indenting South Jersey's pine woods, it works in Oregon's Willamette Valley, and it works most places in between. Sometimes it isn't perfect for the job at hand, but it's a good compromise. The guy who isn't a guncrank can buy such an outfit, use it all his life, and be pretty well satisfied. Nevertheless, other combinations will do equally well under most conditions, which means there is room for personal preference in this game, and there are times when, selected to go with specific situations, others will be superior.

Before getting too involved, perhaps we should take a minute to fill in some basic background for new hunters, to make sure we're all talking the same lingo.

To begin, six different size shotshells are in more or less common use in the U.S. today, the 10-, 12-, 16-, 20-, and 28-gauges, and the .410 bore. (Actually, not many 10s or 28s are seen.) These terms refer basically to the inside diameter of the guns' bores. In the gauges, the smaller the number, the greater the bore diameter. This comes about because the number tells how many balls of that particular size can be obtained from one pound of lead. If you can get 20 balls from a pound, the balls obviously have to be smaller than if you get only 10.

---

* They really mean "high brass." The base of a shotshell is the wad inside the head; its height largely governs powder capacity, thus a "high base" shell has less room for propellant than a low base one and actually refers to a skeet, target or field load, rather than a long range or Magnum load.

The .410 bore is not a gauge, but a caliber. It is the nominal measurement of the inside diameter of the main part of the bore in inches. You can get about 67½ lead balls of .410" diameter from a pound of lead, so this might be called a 67 gauge. As a matter of interest, the 10-gauge in inches measures .775; the 12-gauge, .730; 16-gauge, .670; 20-gauge, .615; and 28-gauge, .550.

Viewed sketchily, a modern shotshell is made up of a plastic case, brass cup, primer, smokeless powder, combination plastic wad column and shotcup, and shot. Some designs have separate base wads of plastic or other material in the head (rear) end of the case, while in other designs this wad is integrally formed with the sidewalls. The base wad strengthens the case and regulates internal volume. The brass cup, made in varying heights, surrounds the head end of the case. The cup was necessary for strength in old-style paper cases and still has some value in this regard in plastics. Its rim also provides good purchase for the gun's extracting mechanism. The face of the brass cup is indented in the center to accept a primer, which is the ignition device of a shell. A small hole leads from the primer pocket into the case. The powder is dumped into the base of the case and held there firmly by the bottom of the wad column/shotcup unit which is shaped to form a gas seal when the powder burns. Collapsible plastic legs connect the gas seal portion to the shotcup. The shotcup is a plastic cup of the proper diameter to fit firmly inside the case; it is deep enough to hold the weight of shot desired and split lengthwise in several places. The shot is the load of pellets which are used as ballistic projectiles. It is contained in the case by crimping the mouth shut with six or eight pie-cut-shaped folds.

A shotshell is activated when the gun's firing pin strikes the primer. That unit contains a chemical mixture which reacts to the blow and sends a squirt of flame through the flash hole to ignite the powder. As the powder burns (It doesn't explode.) it creates gas which, because it is confined, builds up pressure. The pressure intensifies the burning, which in turn increases the gas pressure. Eventually—the time actually is measured in milliseconds—something has to give; if it didn't, the gun would burst. The shell case, supported by the gun's action and its barrel, seals off any significant expansion to the rear or sides, but the shot charge in its plastic cup is moveable, and it squirts down the bore, through the choke, and out the muzzle. As this unit meets the resistance of the atmosphere, the splits in the cup permit the plastic to peel away from the load and quickly drop to the ground, while the shot goes on to form its pattern and, hopefully, center your target.

In times past, shotshells were made in somewhat different ways, of different materials, but there's no need to go into those details here. They also were made in many different lengths, the variations sometimes being so small that it's hard to determine why they were created. Today, there is much more standardization, the .410 coming in two lengths, 2½- and 3-inch, the 28- and 16-gauges in 2¾-inch, and 20- and 12-gauges in 2¾- and 3-inch, the 10-gauge in 2⅞-, 3-, and 3½-inch. Powder charges vary primarily according to the velocity desired and the pressure acceptable with a given weight of shot. Shot weights range, in commercial loads, from one-half ounce in the short .410 through 2 ounces in the Magnum 10-gauge.

Shot sizes in hunting loads range from 9s through BB's, the larger numbers again indicating the smaller diameter. Diameters in hundredths of inches of American-made shot can be determined by subtracting the size number from 17; for example, No. 6 shot is 17 minus 6 or .11 inches in diameter. (This gimmick's use ends with No. 2 shot, as air rifle shot, BB's, and the various sizes of buck shot are larger than .17 inches.) Shot is also made in Nos. 10, 11, and 12, but there is little practical application for these sizes in the field. The smaller sizes obviously give a denser pattern (a term referring to the number of pellets on a target area of given size), but the comparatively light weight of these individual pellets causes them to lose momentum faster than the larger sizes, so they are efficient at only short to medium distances. As the range increases, progressively larger shot are necessary to maintain velocity reasonably well. (A sphere actually is an extremely poor shape for overcoming atmospheric resistance, regardless of size, if it must be small enough to shoot from a shoulder arm.) However, because there are comparatively few large shot in any practical load, the pattern they create loses density rapidly and soon reaches the point where it will not put enough pellets into a gamebird to reliably kill it. Thus the shotgun is, was, and probably always will be a short range firearm. Truth is, few if any shotguns of any gauge, with any load, will consistently kill gamebirds at 70 yards. Not even the 10-gauge Magnum with a 2-oz. load. It's possible to knock pheasants down fairly regularly at that distance. (Breaking a wing is comparatively easy to do.) If a hunter has a good dog which gathers in such birds, he may come to believe he's killing birds at fantastic distances. Actually he's crippling them, and the dog is doing the genuine work. Most broken-wing birds will escape the dogless hunter. Sixty yards is a more realistic maximum range, but only if the gunner is an expert. The average shooter will be well advised to keep his shots well within 50. Even 50 yards is an awfully long shot when we're talking about genuine three-foot-to-the-yard yards. Most hunters who drop a bird at 30 yards call it 40, and the rare 50-yard kill is called 70. This occurs not because most gunners are untruthful but because they simply can't judge range accurately and they always estimate over, never under, like their cousins the fishermen.

The propellant in a modern shotshell is smokeless powder. However, in the earlier shotgunning days, with both muzzle-loader and breech-loader, black powder was used. Except for the fact that both powders can be used to eject a load of shot from a smoothbore barrel, they don't have an awful lot in common. Black powder is centuries old, perhaps 2000 years old, though its use in true guns is much more recent. Smokeless powder is scarcely more than a century old. Black powder is a mechanical mixture of potassium nitrate, charcoal, and sulfur. Smokeless powder is a chemical compound created on a base of nitrated cellulose. Compared to smokeless powder, black powder burns at low pressure.

At the time when black powder was used in shotshells, the charge was measured in drams (In avoirdupois weight, there are 16 drams in an ounce.), and the charge was marked on the shell. When the changeover to smokeless powder came, shooters were used to thinking in terms of "drams of powder," so instead of marking shells with the weight of the new propellant (which was considerably less than that of black powder, as the smokeless delivered more energy per unit of weight), a "dram equivalent" figure was listed. This indicated that the smokeless powder charge, whatever its actual weight, gave the shot charge the same average velocity as would that number of drams of black powder. This made it simple for the hunter to get a smokeless load which would give him the same ballistics as he'd been used to with black powder. The practice is continued today with factory-loaded shotshells, a typical marking of 3¼-1¼-6 indicating an equivalent of 3¼ drams of black powder and 1¼ oz. of No. 6 shot. Shotshell handloaders ignore this drams business completely, using grains as their basic weight, the same as metallic case handloaders of rifle and handgun ammo do. This a much more convenient unit, since its smaller value (7000 grains per pound vs. 256 drams) makes it unnecessary to deal in fractions of an ounce; also because most handloading scales, powder measures, and tool powder bushings are calibrated in grains.

During the transitional period from black to smokeless powder, which occurred prior to the turn of the century, a number of so-called smokeless "bulk" powders were marketed. Handloading with simple tools was common at that time, and these particular smokeless powders were so made that they could be loaded bulk for bulk with black, which simplified the handloading process.

Because smokeless powder burns at a much higher pressure than black, it should never be used in guns designed to work with the old powder. It simply isn't safe.

Shot is usually made of lead, with traces of another element or two to harden it. Lead is the only material now available at a reasonable price which has the physical properties to permit a simple manufacturing process and be reasonably efficient from a ballistic standpoint. Sometimes the pellets are given a copper or nickel plating to reduce deformation in the bore and thus to improve the patterns, but this is largely of interest to advance handloaders only. Of more importance, at least to the waterfowl shooter, is the assumption that great numbers of bottom-feeding ducks and geese die each year of lead poisoning caused by pellets ingested in heavily gunned marshes and other shallow water areas. Currently, much research is being conducted, primarily with ferrous metals, to find a shot material which will eliminate this problem. At this writing, the answer is not in sight. Iron or soft steel shot does not poison ducks, but due to its low density, relative to lead, it is inefficient at the longer ranges at which ducks often are taken. Hopefully, some breakthrough will soon be made in this area. If not, it is questionable whether ferrous shot will actually benefit the overall duck population, for gunners may well cripple and lose as many birds with it, at what would be normal range with lead shot, as will be saved from poisoning. This is no problem to the pheasant hunter, fortunately.

The pattern which will be formed by a load of shot will be determined, for the most part, by the choke in the gun barrel. This is a constriction or narrowing of the inside diameter of the barrel within a few inches of the muzzle or front end. The principle is similar to that of the nozzle on a garden hose. The choke regulates, within limits, the kind of spray you get from your shot pellets, thus it determines pattern size and density at a given distance. Usually, choke is machined into the barrel at the factory, but it is also possible to have an adjustable choke installed on a single-barrel gun so you can manually change patterns between shots.

Until late in the last century, shotgun bores were made the same diameter from just ahead of the chamber to the muzzle. In other words, they were straight cylinders. With this configuration, they would rarely put more than 40 percent of their shot pellets into a 30-inch circle at 40 yards, the distance at which loads normally are tested. With this density, they could not be relied on to kill beyond about 35 yards, as with most loads it takes about 50% pattern to get the required number of pellets in a bird at that distance. Fred Kimble, an American market hunter, often is credited with inventing choke boring, though there is evidence that some English gunmakers were familiar with it at about the same time. At any rate, with barrels so made it soon was possible to obtain patterns of 70% or more, and with these densities birds could be killed regularly to 50 yards or so, assuming the hunter could center that pattern on them.

Patterns of hunting guns are always spoken of as the percentage of the pellets in the total shot load placed in a 30-inch circle at 40 yards. (Skeet guns often are tested at 30 yards.) The 40-yard distance was chosen long ago as standard for hunting guns because it was far enough to show significant holes in patterns but not so far that the patterns had disintegrated too much to be useful.

Beginning with the original unchoked "cylinder" bore which delivered about 40% patterns, the following identifying terms and their average percentages have evolved and been accepted by most shooting authorities:

PATTERN PERCENTAGES OF
DIFFERENT CHOKES AT 40 YARDS

Cylinder	(Cyl)	40%
Skeet #1	(SK 1)	40%
Skeet #2	(SK 2)	50%
Improved Cylinder	(IC)	50%
Modified	(Mod.)	60%
Improved Modified	(IM)	65%
Full		70%

In actual shooting, these percentages are far from exact. If you fire a box of shells and actually count pellet holes and calculate percentages, you might well find a spread of 10 percentage points among them. The barrel which averages modified patterns with one size and weight of shot will sometimes give full, or perhaps improved cylinder, percentages with another shell. There's no way of knowing these things with certainty without testing. In other words, the choke designation stamped on your barrel may be correct with one size, weight and velocity of shot, but the chances are good it won't be correct with all the loads you're likely to run through it, and maybe not even with one. This can make a great difference in your hitting ability. If you believe you're getting IC patterns but actually they're full choke, you'll either be missing most of those close-flushing woodcock and grouse or chopping them up completely.

The choke subject was greatly complicated by the development of the plastic shotcup wad unit. This unit definitely tightens patterns, and the hunter who uses shells having plastic shotcups in a gun manufactured before they came into common use finds himself way overchoked. The general effect of the shotcup is to add a full degree of choke to a barrel. That is, a barrel that gives improved cylinder patterns with old shells (no shotcups and probably an overshot wad rather than today's pie crimp) will likely get modified patterns from the new shells. Or a modified bore will probably give full choke patterns.

Newer guns—those manufactured since the takeover of the shotcup shells—don't have this problem, for they are choked to accommodate for it. As the shell's efficiency was increased (if the

Many shots at roosters come at short range when flushed by a retriever or kicked out by the hunter.

ability to deliver more dense patterns can be considered an improvement), the choke machined into the gun's bore was slackened so that the overall effect was to continue giving 70% average patterns for full choke guns, 60% for modified, etc. If nothing else, this was a practical approach, for the vast majority of shotgun kills are made at short to medium range, where fairly open patterns are more effective than ultra-tight ones, but it is ironic that the most useful device to tighten patterns since the development of the choked barrel actually is of little real use to most hunters.

Though pattern percentages are normally given at 40 yards, it's obvious that at closer ranges they will be denser and at longer ranges more open. On a rough average, you will gain 8 to 10 percent in density for each 5-yard decrease in range and lose that percentage for each 5-yard increase. Thus the 50% IC pattern at 40 yards becomes a 70% "full" choke at 30, and the 70% full choke at 40 yards becomes the 50% "improved cylinder" at 50. Some full choke guns actually deliver 80% or better patterns at 40 yards, so their maximum efficient range is in excess of 50 yards, but it's hard to make an argument for any shotgun as a 70-yard killer. Everybody occasionally makes longer kills (I once dropped a crow at 87 measured yards with a light load of 7½s.), but these are the results of chance and such shooting should be discouraged. It leads to too many cripples that fly on to die wastefully.

Pattern percentages are figured the same for all gauges. If you have a 20-gauge Magnum giving 70% patterns with 1¼ oz. of No. 6 shot, it will kill just as well and as far as a 12-gauge using an identical load and getting the same average pattern. The 12-gauge might have a theoretical edge due to a bit more velocity. (The larger the gauge, the higher the velocity within a given class of loadings such as "long range," "field," "target," etc., as assembled by various manufacturers.) However, differences in killing power resulting from velocity variations within normal loadings are insignificant in the field. In the not-distant past it probably was easier to get high-percentage patterns from a 12-gauge than from a 20-gauge, because fewer pellets in a given weight charge came into contact with the larger bore as the shot moved down the barrel, thus fewer were deformed by friction to be squirted off at odd angles when they met the resistance of the atmosphere. The plastic shotcups largely eliminated such deformation. There probably is still some pellet deformation when the sudden blow of the expanding powder gases strikes the bottom of the shot charge and begins to shove it ahead before the top pellets start to move, but this is common to all gauges. It seems likely that the 12-gauge would offend more in this regard than the 20-gauge, for more pellets are exposed to the gas's effect due to the larger cross-sectional area of the 12's bore and because its shot charge has less depth in which to absorb the impact. Burning rates of powders have an effect here also, with the edge going to 20 because it usually is loaded with more progressive burning types that apply their force more gradually. In the final analysis, however, such quibbles are unimportant to the average hunter who is largely unconcerned as to *why* something happens, so long as he knows it *does* happen. And of course the pattern percentage figure takes all these things into account; if a given weight of a certain size shot pellet gives a 70% pattern out of a certain gun, so far as killing power is concerned it doesn't matter in the slightest what gauge that gun is.

In a standard-length 20-ga. shell, the author prefers 1⅛ oz. of 7½s in the modified barrel of his M21 Winchester, and the same weight of 6s in the full choke tube, both in high-velocity loading. In the 3-inch 20-ga. Magnum, 1¼ oz. of shot makes an even better long range load.

So what does it take to reliably kill pheasants? You'll recall Major Burrard's basic criterion was three English No. 6 pellets in the 17+ square inches of vital area. Francis Sell advised four hits somewhere on the body (which will average two in the vital area) with individual pellet energy of 2 foot pounds, or six to eight hits with 1¼ to 1½ foot pounds, and this is in line with Jack O'Connor's thinking. It's interesting to note that these authorities, and many others, almost invariably speak of multiple hits. This suggests that total kinetic energy alone is not an accurate way of determining shot charge effectiveness; i.e., a single No. 2 pellet may have more energy at 40 yards than two No. 5s, yet the two 5s would probably kill better. I doubt if anyone is certain why this is so, but experience indicates that it is. It may be due to the increased chance of delivering at least part of the energy to a truly vital spot. It may be due to the fact that various parts of the bird's body are affected at the same instant, in a sense overpowering more of the creature's life forces than a single pellet, even though that pellet might do more local damage. It might be due to a "summation" effect by which the applied energy of the several pellets somehow surpasses their mathematical kinetic energy. There might be other reasons no one has even guessed at. I don't know. Direct observation by numerous hunters over periods of some generations insists, however, that multiple hits are superior to a single one, even when their kinetic energies are very close.

Because ducks allegedly are harder to kill than pheasants (I often think a duck hunter originated that statement; I haven't found it to

What to Hit Him With . . . the Ammo

be so, but my duck shooting experience is limited so to save argument I'll accept it for now.), we need slightly less energy to kill ringnecks consistently than is needed for ducks of about the same size. If Sell's six to eight body hits with each pellet having 1¼ to 1½ foot pounds of energy is correct for average duck shooting, perhaps we can settle for six body hits (or three in the true vital area) with about 1¼ foot pounds of energy each for pheasants, a total of 3¾-4 foot pounds. The thing now is to determine at what distance given loads of shot will give the required pattern density and pellet energy.

Table 1, nearby, lists common loads and muzzle velocities for the various gauges. Others are available—the 3½-inch 10-gauge Magnum using 5 DE (drams equivalent) of powder and 2 oz. of No. 2s, for instance—but they aren't too practical as pheasant loads. Many "field" loads are offered in the three common gauges, and these are practical for pheasants under many conditions.

Table 2 gives the approximate number of pellets of Nos. 2, 3, 4, 5, 6, and 7½ shot in charge weights from ¾ oz. to 1⅞ oz. This covers all loads normally thought of as suitable for pheasants, and includes

Table 1

Gauge	Shell Length	Powder DE	Shot Oz.	Shot Sizes	Muzzle Vel. FPS
10	2⅞	4¾	1⅝	2, 4	1330
12	3	4¼	1⅝	2, 4, 5, 6	1315
12	3	4	1⅜	2, 4, 6	1315
12	2¾	4	1½	2, 4, 6	1315
12	2¾	3¾	1¼	2, 4, 5, 6, 7½	1330
16	2¾	3½	1¼	2, 4, 6	1295
16	2¾	3¼	1⅛	2, 4, 5, 6, 7½	1295
20	3	3¼	1¼	4, 6, 7½	
20	2¾	3	1⅛	2, 4, 6	1220
20	2¾	2¾	1	2, 4, 5, 6, 7½	1220
28	2¾	2¼	⅞	4, 6, 7½	1295
28	2¾	2¼	¾	6, 7½	1295
410	3	Max	¾	6, 7½	1135

Table 2

Approximate Number of Pellets in Selected Shot Charges

Shot Size	Shot Charge Weight (Ounces)											
	3/4	7/8	1	1 1/16	1 1/8	1 3/16	1 1/4	1 3/8	1 1/2	1 5/8	1 3/4	1 7/8
2		79	90	96	102	108	113	124	135	146	157	169
3		93	106	113	119	126	133	146	160	172	185	199
4		118	135	144	152	161	169	186	203	220	237	253
5		149	170	181	191	202	213	234	255	276	297	319
6	169	197	225	239	253	267	281	309	338	366	394	422
7½	263	303	350	374	397	421	444	492	525	586	633	566

some which rarely if ever would be used, such as the heavy charges of small shot. These totals are given as a matter of interest, not because they are practical loads.

Table 3 shows these various weights with the common shot sizes; the number of pellets which average improved cylinder, modified, and full chokes will give in the traditional 30-inch circle at 40 yards; and the number of pellets these chokes will place in Burrard's 17+ square-inch vital area of a 2½-lb. pheasant at ranges from 30 to 60 yards. These average hits were determined by calculating the pellets per square inch placed by the given chokes in the 30-inch circle (which contains some 707 square inches), and relating this to the square inches in the vital area. Results at ranges other than 40 yards were calculated by adding 10% for each 5-yard decrease in range, deducting 10% for each 5-yard increase.

Table 4 lists remaining velocities at 20, 40, and 60 yards, and energies for common shot sizes at 20, 30, 40, 50, and 60 yards, beginning with a high (1330 fps), a medium (1220 fps), and a low (1135 fps) muzzle velocity.

It's interesting to note that increased velocity, at least of the magnitude practical in shotshells, has little effect on kinetic energy at the longer ranges. For example, a No. 4 shot started at 1330 feet per second has but 685 fps remaining at 60 yards, while the same size

Table 3

Shot Charge and Total Pellets	Choke	Pellets in 30" circle 40 yds.	Pellets in 17+ sq. in. vital area of 2½-lb. pheasant at these yardages:			
			30	40	50	60
¾ oz. No. 6 (169)	70%	118	3.6	2.8	2	
¾ oz. No. 7½ (263)	70%	184	5.7	4.4	3.1	
⅞ oz. No. 6 (197)	60%	118	3.8	2.8	1.9	
	70%	138	4.2	3.3	2.4	
⅞ oz. No. 7½ (303)	60%	182	5.8	4.4	2.9	
	70%	212	6.6	5.1	3.6	
1 oz. No. 4 (135)	50%	68	2.3	1.6		
	60%	81	2.6	1.9	1.3	
	70%	95	2.9	2.3	1.6	
1 oz. No. 5 (170)	50%	85	2.9	2.0	1.2	
	60%	102	3.3	2.4	1.6	
	70%	119	3.7	2.9	2.0	
1 oz. No. 6 (225)	50%	113	3.8	2.7	1.6	
	60%	135	4.3	3.2	2.2	
	70%	158	4.8	3.8	2.7	
1 oz. No. 7½ (350)	50%	175	5.9	4.2	2.5	
	60%	210	6.7	·5	3.4	
	70%	245	7.6	5.9	4.2	2.5
1⅛ oz. No. 4 (152)	50%	76	2.5	1.8	1.1	
	60%	91	2.9	2.2	1.5	
	70%	106	3.3	2.5	1.8	1.1
1⅛ oz. No.5 (191)	50%	96	3.2	2.3	1.4	
	60%	115	3.7	2.8	1.8	
	70%	134	4.1	3.2	2.3	1.4
1⅛ oz. No. 6 (253)	50%	127	4.2	3	1.8	
	60%	152	4.8	3.6	2.4	
	70%	177	5.5	4.2	3	1.8
1⅛ oz. No. 7½ (397)	50%	199	6.7	4.8	2.9	
	60%	238	7.6	5.7	3.8	1.9
	70%	278	8.6	6.7	4.8	2.9

Table 3

Shot Charge and Total Pellets	Choke	Pellets in 30" circle 40 yds.	Pellets in 17+ sq. in. vital area of 2½-lb. pheasant at these yardages:			
			30	40	50	60
1¼ oz. No. 4 (169)	50%	85	2.8	2	1.2	
	60%	101	3.2	2.4	1.6	
	70%	118	3.6	2.8	2	1.2
1¼ oz. No. 5 (213)	50%	107	3.6	2.6	1.5	
	60%	128	4.1	3.1	2	
	70%	149	4.6	3.6	2.6	1.5
1¼ oz. No. 6 (281)	50%	141	4.7	3.4	2	
	60%	169	5.4	4.1	2.7	1.3
	70%	197	6	4.7	3.4	2
1¼ oz. No. 7½ (444)	50%	222	7.5	5.3	3.2	1
	60%	266	8.5	6.4	4.3	2.1
	70%	311	9.6	7.5	5.3	3.2
1⅜ oz. No. 4 (186)	50%	93	3.1	2.2	1.3	
	60%	112	3.6	2.7	1.8	
	70%	130	4	3.1	2.2	1.3
1⅜ oz. No. 6 (309)	50%	155	5.2	3.7	2.2	
	60%	185	5.9	4.5	3	1.5
	70%	216	6.7	5.2	3.7	2.2
1½ oz. No. 4 (203)	50%	102	3.4	2.4	1.4	
	60%	122	3.9	2.9	1.9	
	70%	142	4.4	3.4	2.4	1.4
1½ oz. No. 5 (255)	50%	128	4.3	3.1	1.8	
	60%	153	4.9	3.7	2.4	
	70%	179	5.5	4.3	3.1	1.8
1½ oz. No. 6 (338)	50%	169	5.7	4.1	2.4	
	60%	203	6.5	5.9	3.2	1.6
	70%	237	7.3	5.7	4.1	2.4
1⅝ oz. No. 4 (220)	50%	110	3.7	2.6	1.6	
	60%	132	4.2	3.1	2.1	
	70%	154	4.8	3.7	2.6	1.6
1⅝ oz. No. 5 (276)	50%	138	4.6	3.3	2	
	60%	166	5.3	4	2.6	1.3
	70%	193	6	4.6	3.3	2

Table 3

Shot Charge and Total Pellets	Choke	Pellets in 30" circle 40 yds.	Pellets in 17+ sq. in. vital area of 2½-lb. pheasant at these yardages:			
			30	40	50	60
1⅝ oz. No. 6	50%	183	6.1	4.4	2.6	1.6
(366)	60%	220	7	5.2	3.5	1.7
	70%	256	7.9	6.1	4.4	2.6
1⅞ oz. No. 4	50%	127	4.2	3	1.8	
(253)	60%	152	4.8	3.6	2.4	
	70%	177	5.4	4.2	3	1.8

Table 4
Velocity and Energy of Shot

Muzzle Velocity	Shot Size	Approx. velocity in fps at:			Approx. energy in fp per pellet at:				
		20	40	60	20	30	40	50	60
1330 fps	2	1045	860	730	11.8	9.5	8.0	6.8	5.8
	4	1010	815	685	7.3	6.0	4.8	4.0	3.4
	5	990	790	655	5.6	4.5	3.6	3.0	2.5
	6	970	765	630	4.0	3.0	2.5	2.0	1.7
	7½	930	715	580	2.4	1.9	1.4	1.1	.9
1220 fps	2	975	815	695	10.3	8.6	7.1	6.1	5.2
	4	945	775	655	6.4	5.3	4.3	3.6	3.0
	5	930	750	630	4.9	4.0	3.2	2.7	2.3
	6	910	725	605	3.6	2.9	2.3	1.9	1.6
	7½	875	680	560	2.1	1.7	1.3	1.1	.9
1135 fps	4	895	740	630	5.7	4.7	3.9	3.2	2.8
	5	880	715	605	4.4	3.6	2.9	2.4	2.1
	6	860	695	580	3.2	2.6	2.1	1.7	1.5
	7½	830	655	540	1.9	1.5	1.2	1.0	.8

started at 1135 fps, almost 200 fps slower, reaches the 60-yard mark with 630 fps; it has closed the 195-fps gap to 55 fps. This comes about because atmospheric resistance varies as the square of the velocity; therefore, higher velocity projectiles encounter more resistance than lower velocity ones and lose velocity more rapidly. In practical terms this means that the high velocity loads deliver their significantly more powerful results at short distances, where the excess probably isn't needed because patterns are naturally denser. At the longer ranges, where the shooter might expect to gain through their use, they offer little real advantage except a slightly faster time of flight (despite the fact that they lose velocity faster, they still get there quicker) and somewhat less drop (about 2 inches less over 60 yards, in the case of No. 4s, an amount that is swallowed up by normal pattern dispersion).

Working with the tables we get some interesting conclusions, and some of these seem contrary to common sense. As an example, according to these figures a maximum-loaded, three-inch .410 using ¾ oz. of No. 6 shot from a full choke barrel should put two or three pellets into the vital area of a pheasant at 40 yards. Because each of these pellets has approximately 2.1 foot pounds of energy at that distance, we should be crowding close to consistent kills. Yet scads of field experience shows that the .410 can not be counted on to kill regularly at 40 yards or even at 35 yards. Many veteran hunters claim 25 yards is about its effective limit. Why? All the reasons aren't known, but one is that it's very difficult to get the 70% patterns from the .410's long, skinny shot charge that are required to give the necessary hits. Another possibility is that in the .410 the ¾ oz. load doesn't actually contain ¾ oz. of shot.

Another problem is that there's no way of knowing when those two or three No. 6 pellets arrive at the target. The pattern from any shot charge is not truly pie-pan shaped, as it might appear on a board, but is actually strung out in an elongated mass (remember the comparision to a hoze nozzle?) which at a distance of 50 yards from the gun may be a dozen or more feet long, from the leading pellets to the rearmost ones. This means that if fired at a target moving at an angle to the shot, the bird might be struck in the vital area by a "front-running" pellet but pass out of the pattern's perimeter before the second pellet (which would have registered in the vital area of a motionless target) arrives. This is one reason results shown on a patterning board cannot be implicitly believed. They do not take into account the length of the shot string. Shotshell manufacturers strive to produce shells which deliver short shot strings, for the nearer the pattern approaches the theoretically ideal circular shape, the more pellets will be put into a target moving across the shooter's front. This of course assumes that the shooter is going to place his pattern perfectly. It's possible that a shooter will sometimes lead a target too much, in which case the front pellets will pass beyond the target before it arrives at the intersection point of his shot charge and the bird's flight path; however, in such a case it might be killed by the trailing pellets which arrive late.

These examples indicate that all tables such as these should be studied for whatever help they can give, but not accepted totally and blindly simply because they are printed in impressive form in a book. Sometimes practicalities are more important than mathematics. If there are cases where a large number of accurately observed field results differ from the tables, be cautious about believing the tables. Your own conclusions, if properly and objectively arrived at, are important too. After all, these tables are only based on observations of other hunters. Yet, at the same time it should be remembered that these hunters are persons of tremendous experience—far more than the average shooter will ever acquire—so their conclusions ought to be considered seriously by anyone truly interested in determining the practical effective range of a given load from a given choke.

Table 3 also is inaccurate to the degree that certain hits-by-pellets results are not shown by a whole number. Obviously, a bird or a section of a patterning board cannot be hit by, say, 2.8 pellets. Such a number is mathematically derived, and on a given shot that given area of target would be struck by either 2 or 3 pellets; 8 out of 10 shots delivering 3 pellets, on the average, and 2 out of 10 shots delivering 2 pellets. Nobody knows in what order these pellet totals would vary, and this helps to explain how one shot will give a clean kill at a certain distance while another one will not. A single pellet might not seem significant when you're used to thinking in terms of the hundreds in a load, but at the longer gamebird ranges only a few pellets are actually working for you, and going from 2 hits to 3 is a 50% increase in killing power.

Pheasants are big tough birds, and many experienced hunters such as Chick Holmes prefer heavy loads of 5s or 6s and a tightly bored gun for all their shooting, but desirable as these are for the longer shots, the author likes the denser patterns of 7½s at short range.

Once we get above the .410, it's easier to get high-percentage patterns, and the tables indicate that a modified (60%) 28-gauge using ⅞ oz. of No. 6 shot will handle pheasants to almost 40 yards, while a full choke (70%) barrel will add about five yards to that. It would seem the same weight of No. 7½ ought to give about the same effective ranges, because the decreased energy of this small shot should be balanced by an increase in hits. However, field experience indicates that No. 7½ shot has acceptable penetration on the pheasant's hard feathers to only about 35 to 40 yards, so even multiple pellets on target beyond that distance do not always kill well unless the head or neck is hit. If we go to 1 oz. of No. 4, as in a 20-gauge load, it takes at least a modified barrel, and preferably a full choke, to be consistent at only 30 yards, due to the skimpy pattern. No. 5s from a full choke make a 40-yard outfit, and an ounce of 6s from a 70 percent tube will take pheasants to about 50 yards. No. 7½ of course gives more striking pellets than No. 6, but the remaining energies are such that No. 6 proves a better choice, except at the shorter ranges.

Increasing shot charge weight increases the chances of getting multiple hits on the vital area at any range, but the interworking characteristics of pattern density and kinetic energy show that it's difficult to get a load which will kill consistently at 60 yards. At that distance it takes at least 1½ oz. of No. 6 to insure multiple hits with fair frequency, even from a 70% barrel. And it takes multiple hits to insure kills, for at 60 yards a No. 6 shot started at the high muzzle velocity of 1330 fps has a remaining energy of only 1.7 fp.

If we go to small shot we can increase the number of hits, but the

What to Hit Him With . . . the Ammo

energy is lacking. With 1¼ oz. of No. 7½, we would get 3 or more hits from a full choke, but energy would be only 0.9 fp per pellet, which doesn't add up high enough. Going to 1¼ oz. of No. 5 from a 70% barrel averages 1.5 hits at 2.5 fp per pellet. This means that even on the shots which deliver 2 pellets at 5 fp, we'd have only a fair chance of killing. The 1¼ oz. load of No. 6, full choke, will give 2 hits and 3.4 fp—another maybe. Even going to high velocity, heavy shot charge loads such as 1½ oz. of No. 6 or 1⅝ oz. of No. 5 from a 70% barrel can not guarantee unfailing consistency on 60-yard pheasants of the 2½-lb. size we've been discussing.

Undoubtedly many pheasants are killed each season at ranges exceeding 60 yards (and many times this number are hit, but not well enough to drop them, and they fly on to become fox food). The kills can be accounted for in several ways. Probably the most important one is luck. Random placement puts a pellet or two into a quick-kill spot. If enough chances are taken at 70- and 80-yard birds, a certain percentage has to be killed outright, but such results are due to pure chance and nobody should take credit for his shooting ability on such shots. Another explanation is the fact that some guns and loads pattern more tightly than the maximum 70% we've been discussing. Actually, 80% combinations are not rare (though they aren't too plentiful either), and 85–90% outfits occur. One of these, in the hands of a super marksman, can add some distance to the 60-yard maximum we've arrived at. But experts who can handle these guns are mighty few and far between. I'm not one of them, and I have a hunch you aren't either. As members of a select and blessed group, these people are best considered as near-gods to be admired and pondered from afar, rather than as ordinary mortals whose abilities should be emulated. Until you can break, say, 80% of your trap targets from the 27-yard line, it's best to confine your live bird shooting to less than 50 yards and preferably ten yards less. Results over the long haul will be much more satisfying, for you'll know you've consigned far fewer pheasants to the foxes.

So after all the figures are figured, is there an answer to the question raised near the beginning of this chapter: "What's the best load for pheasants?" Well, maybe.

If I had to go with just one load from here on out, it would be a high velocity shell using 1¼ oz. of No. 6 shot. It's available in 20-, 16-,

A high velocity load of 1¼ oz. of 6s is available in all common gauges and, everything considered, this seems the best choice if a hunter is going to shoot all his pheasants with one load.

and 12-gauge, and it will consistently handle pheasants to 40 yards with an improved cylinder barrel, to about 45 with a modified, and to better than 50 yards with a full choke. That takes in all of my normal shooting. The only time I shoot at a rooster farther away than this is when I make a mistake about range or a hit bird is trying to get away. A case could be made for 1¼ oz. or 5s, but I can't see any need for going bigger. Smaller sizes don't perform consistently at the longer ranges. My own field experience suggests 6s make the best compromise between number of hits and energy per pellet. When most shooting is at short to medium range, the high velocity loads are not necessary, but where the last bit of energy is needed, they do provide a slight advantage. It takes a 1½ oz. or heavier load of 6s from a full choke barrel to make just a reasonably consistent 60-yard pheasant killer, and this gets into the 12-gauge Magnum category, where gun weight and handling become problems. Everything considered, it seems the high velocity load with 1¼ oz. of 6s is the best single choice for pheasants in all three common gauges.

What to Hit Him With . . . the Ammo

7

What to Hit Him With —the Gun

The typical pheasant gun is a 12-gauge slide action or autoloader with a 28-inch barrel bored modified or full. There's little doubt of that. The older a hunter is, the better the chance he'll be shooting a long-barreled, tightly choked gun, and a hike through any pheasant cover is still likely to disclose a good percentage of such outfits, though younger hunters are tending away from them.

Slide actions, often called pumps, reached a high state of development just before the turn of the century, the exposed-hammer M97 Winchester being the ultimate for the time. It's not unusual to see one of these old "knuckle-skinners" downing birds yet today, its bluing completely gone, metal parts buffed to a silver-gray patina by decades of use (even the rust spots are polished smooth), all finish and checkering gone from the woodwork, simply obliterated by the handling, weather, cornstalk contact, and all the other little bits and pieces of pheasant hunting that expose the character of a real hunting gun. Lord A'mighty, what stories these old guns could tell, could we but understand their speech. . .

The old 97 wasn't the first repeater used in American gamefields. A decade earlier, Winchester offered the lever action smoothbore M87 in 10- and 12-gauge, apparently a spin-off of the successful lever action rifles then, and still, so popular. I never even saw one of those early guns, though I almost bought a M1901 (a M1887 revamped for smokeless powder) from Charley Evens, New Meadows, Idaho, gunsmith, when batting the breeze with him one day in the late '40s. It was an interesting design, but as much as I liked lever rifles in those days, it didn't seem a natural way to manipulate a smoothbore. Winchester's M93 effected the switch from the lever approach to the slide action and was itself superseded by the M97, which then in turn gave way to the gun that's been called, perhaps correctly, the perfect repeater, the Model 12 Winchester. I wouldn't want to say that no other slide action ever equaled the M12, but I rather doubt if there's been a better one.

About the same time the M12 came along, John Browning perfected his autoloading shotgun. It had a lot in common with the slide action: large magazine capacity for the firepower that came in handy during the days of large limits; the single sighting plane which a lot of shooters came to prefer; a single trigger rather than the two that were common on doubles of that day, which made it easy to get a proper, no-compromise stock length; and a hand-filling fore-end to give good gun control. The Browning went one step further than the Winchester. It completely eliminated the necessity for manual operation of the action to reload. The slide action utilized a simple movement of the forward hand to eject the empty case and run a loaded one into the chamber, a highly efficient procedure, but the Browning took advantage of part of the energy resulting from the firing of the shell itself to get rid of that empty and ram a new load home. Most early repeaters had magazines that would handle four shells, with a fifth in the chamber, a design that still endures with many despite the fact that federal and state laws often restrict them to a three-shell total to reduce their deadliness. Even so, that's still 50 percent more than you can safely stuff in any double gun and so remains a fact that influences many buyers.

As time went on, the single-barrel repeaters were made even more versatile by the development of adjustable chokes. These let the hunter adapt his boring, either by exchange of different-size tubes or a simple twist of the wrist with a collet-type choke, so that he could handle grouse and woodcock in thick cover or pheasants and ducks at long range. The efficiency of such designs could not be

Hunters discussing which way to make next sweep are carrying typical —if different—pheasant guns. Bob Bell, left, with 20-ga. Winchester double, Jim Bashline and an over/under, and Harry Plitt with a 12-ga. autoloader.

ignored, especially in a country like ours whose national mentality seems to revolve on such catch phrases as "firstest with the mostest," "hit 'em again . . . harder," and "if it's bigger (or more numerous) it's better."

All these characteristics contributed to the popularity of autoloaders and slide actions with Americans. This popularity still continues, basically for one reason in additon to those mentioned: these guns work. If everything in this world worked as well as an old Model 12 Winchester or a Browning 5-shot autoloader, we'd be so efficient we couldn't stand each other. If any two-word description fits guns like these, it's "shooting machines." I speak from personal experience. Many years ago, my father gave me a "sweet sixteen" Browning autoloader with 26-inch, vent-rib barrel bored improved cylinder. I used it for most of my upland shooting for two decades and found it nearly perfect, though I was bothered by its comparatively long length for the short barrel and somewhere along the way had a Poly-Choke installed to give an overall barrel length of 22 inches. Though certainly not a pretty outfit (my shooting friends called it "Old Ugly", but I call it my "meat gun"), it was, and is, a deadly one, perhaps the most efficient game getter I've ever used. There have been seasons in which I killed everything I shot at with it, something I've never done with another gun. I didn't always hit with the first shot, but that's why you carry a repeater, so you can keep on hitting the go-button if necessary. On one occasion I stopped a cottontail on the fourth shot. In an expert display of poor shooting I had missed it three times while it skittered around in thick weeds, and then, as it dove into a narrow fencerow, dropped a shell into the open port, pressed the button that slams the bolt home, and popped the bunny as it cleared the far side of the fencerow. When the action died down and I had time to ponder this episode a bit, I sort of wished I hadn't taken that last shot, as I'd already had more opportunities than anyone could normally ask of a game animal. But during all the excitement, and there are times when even a common cottontail rabbit provides plenty, the thought never occurred to me. At any rate, the episode illustrates the efficiency of these single barrel repeaters and helps to explain their popularity.

This attitude is understandable, maybe even necessary, under some conditions. When hunters were comparatively few and wildlife made up a bigger proportion of the food on the table than it does now, it was natural to use the tool that made the job easiest. The repeating shotgun filled a niche. The fact that it maintained its popularity even after the increased number of hunters and decreased bag limits made it unnecessary, is easily explained. A son grew up watching his father leave the house with his old cornsheller and come home with a canvas coat bulging; it was only natural that when the boy reached hunting age he would emulate his dad. In most cases, of course, the father purchased the youngster's gun; and why wouldn't he get another similar to the one which had served him so well? In other cases, the son simply inherited his dad's gun. After all, these things just aren't worn out by a single lifetime of hunting. As a result, we had several gunning generations in which the vast majority used a shotgun which was some kind of repeater. Even today that

A longtime favorite pheasant gun of Bell's is this Browning sweet sixteen autoloader. With stock tailored to fit and barrel shortened to 22 inches including the Poly-Choke, it's a deadly outfit.

trend holds, and there's nothing wrong with it. These general designs of guns have reached a state of near mechanical perfection. They perform flawlessly in the field, and the game laws which govern bag limits eliminate any aura of "hoggishness" they might have acquired in the early days when restrictions were fewer. A sportsman is a sportsman no matter what gun he prefers, while a person who wants only to kill will be a game hog with anything, be it a single shot .410 or even a slingshot.

Despite their useful design features and efficiency, the autoloaders and pumps are not without faults. The most obvious ones are physical: for a given barrel length they are considerably longer than a double (the full length of the action has to fit between the barrel and the stock), and they are on the heavy side. Another problem, though resulting from the physical makeup, is not simply a matter of inches or pounds but rather a largely subjective thing which some people speak of as "balance." I don't like this word, for it's obvious that any physical item has a balance point which can be determined, yet finding it in a gun doesn't do a great deal toward describing its handling qualities, and these are what we're really interested in. A more descriptive word is "feel," which suggests the interrelationship between the man and the gun, even when both are at rest but most especially when that inanimate metal-and-wood object is expected to respond to the gunner's wishes. Two guns can be the same length, the same weight, yet be completely different in their handling qualities. One will stubbornly resist everything the shooter wants to do, like a partisan fighting a never-ending delaying action, while the other seems to read the gunner's mind—even anticipate it—and with a will of its own is gliding into shooting position even as a flushing bird registers on the hunter's optic and auditory nerves. It's in the feel that the autos and pumps lack something that good doubles have. I'm not certain what is is. I've heard others discuss it, and I've read many observations on it, but I've never known it to be truly and objectively explained. I can't explain it myself. It obviously has to do with the relationships of the various gun parts to the whole, the weights, shapes, and sizes of each item, possibly even the materials they're made of. Perhaps it could be explained in words if enough time and space were devoted to it, but this approach would end up in technical jargon that no one could really appreciate anyhow. How do you translate terms like "vector," "moment of force," and "inertia" into mental images that will accurately reveal a gun's responsiveness? It's much simpler to just handle the guns and feel the difference.

This is not to say that acceptable, even outstanding, shooting cannot be done with repeaters. It can in both the field and on the claybird ranges, but experience indicates that any hunter who uses a good double gun a reasonable length of time will come to realize that it has qualities no other design can equal. He may start with a prejudice against it, as I did after growing up shooting slide actions and autoloaders. However, in some subtle way, without his even realizing it, he'll find that the double has insinuated its way into his affections and without consciously thinking about it he's already relegated, mentally at least, his repeater to standby status.

The choice sometimes has to overcome very practical problems. Back in high school days, my 20-gauge M17 Remington had given way to another fine slide action, a 16-gauge M37 Ithaca. But even then I was eyeing up the twin-tube jobs, particularly Dad's little 16-gauge L. C. Smith. With his permission, I used it one day when he couldn't hunt and promptly found myself all bolloxed up when a bird went out. To begin with, I couldn't find the safety. I was used to shoving off the safety on my pump gun with my trigger finger, and by the time I got untangled and thumbed off the tang safety the rooster was out so far that I hurried the shot and missed clean. Upon which I almost shortened those 26-inch barrels another half-foot, because I pulled on them so hard trying to operate a pump handle that wasn't there. It eventually dawned on me that something wasn't cooperating and after awhile I got around to the rear trigger, but by then the chance was hopeless. So my first hunting experience with a double gun was a bit pathetic. Nevertheless, the sheer delight it gave me to simply carry that little gun and the ease with which I could swing it made it inevitable that I'd have something similar some day. And that's what usually happens to anyone who tries a good double. He ends up hunting with one.

Even in the early part of this century, repeaters weren't the only guns in our pheasant country, even if they did fit there like a wool-socked foot in an old leather boot. There were the single barrels—mostly 12-gauges with long barrels and exposed hammers—that kids liked because they were cheap and farmers liked because they could drop the biggest pheasant that ever squawked, endure years of neglect, and yet function reliably. When one stood behind the kitchen door they made it unnecessary to worry if a tramp (or even John Dillinger) came knocking. There were the double barrels; inexpensive ones made for mail-order trade, and others like the Fox, Lefever, L. C. Smith, Ithaca, Winchester, and Parker, which, in their top grades, did not have to take a back seat to any smoothbores built anywhere.

If the single barrels were popular because they were both cheap and good utility guns, the high-grade doubles maintained their niche because they were, simply, great guns. They were comparatively expensive to manufacture, and this limited their sales possibilities, for there have always been more people of average means than of affluence. This in itself is a selling point with a certain percentage of buyers. There are those who often are ignorant of the genuine reasons for a given firearm's price but who want it because it costs more than an ordinary hunter can afford. Guys like that rub me wrong, but my basic feeling toward them is pity. They can have a true work of art—or maybe a dozen of them—standing in a gun cabinet and be no more aware of it than the man in the moon. Fortunately, they form a small minority. Most gunners cherish a fine double and realize their good fortune in having such a shooting pardner. I doubt if a day afield goes by that they don't, at least subconsciously, give thanks for their luck. If a few do buy them because they're expensive—for their snob appeal, we might say—countless others buy them because they're the only guns that will cool the burning in their souls.

What gives fine doubles this aura? To begin with, we have to admit that part of it is in the mind. We learn, through reading, conversation, observation, or whatever, that certain persons whom we admire or respect prefer doubles to repeaters. Whether we consciously copy them or not, we are influenced by them. There's something about the fact that a tweed-clad, upper-crust Englishman drops driven grouse with a matched pair of Purdeys, Churchills, or Holland & Hollands that affects us. It may be a negative reaction at first. The very fact that royalty and others of vast wealth and influence use doubles for what seems to Americans an artificial type of hunting at best is reason enough for some of us to be repelled by that style of gun. American and British hunting philosophies are not the same. The differing viewpoints of King George III and an American rifleman of the Revolutionary War still exist to some extent and doubtless always will. Yet it's quite likely that far more Americans feel reasonable regard and admiration, rather than dislike, for things British. Even among those who are antagonistic, honesty can make respect necessary, and because no one can deny the ability of the English at their particular shooting games, and as they favor high-grade doubles almost to the exclusion of repeaters, we have to ask ourselves why. We further have to ask why many of our own American shooting experts prefer double guns; not only the well-known gunwriters like Elmer Keith, Jack O'Connor, Warren Page, Francis Sell, and others of their experience and ability, but also the less-known but perhaps even deadlier gunners who do the shooting honors at meets like the National Springer Spaniel Championships, the live-bird "money" competitors, and many local "top guns" who have made their reputation in the same thick covers where you and I do our gunning. Why do shooters like these, pros or semi-pros by our standards, men who could have any make and style of gun in the world, prefer doubles? It's not a mental attitude with them. They're the leaders, not the followers.

There are different reasons, and these are of varying degrees of importance. One is safety. When a double gun is broken, anyone to whom it is visible can tell at a glance it cannot be fired, thus he knows he has nothing to fear from an accidental discharge. This is a factor that should not be taken lightly. A few persons are accidentally shot while hunting every season, and even though the percentage is extremely low, it's still too high, and particularly so if you are one of the statistics. The more a person is around guns, the more he respects them. It's only the nitwit neophyte that acts the fool with either a loaded or an empty gun.

Double guns are often credited with a high degree of reliability, compared with other types, but this is open to question. There's considerable truth to the statement that if two triggers are utilized you then have in effect two single-barrel guns joined into one unit. Each has a separate lock, which means it's possible that one side can go on working even if something such as a broken spring puts the other side out of commission. In actual practice, this isn't always the case as a broken piece from one lock sometimes fouls the other, in which case the gun is out of action.

Many of today's doubles feature single triggers and these, due to their comparatively complicated design, are a bit more likely to give trouble than double triggers. It's fashionable to say that they have reached such a high state of development that they are completely reliable, but even in my limited experience this isn't so. I've had them double, or fire both barrels with a single trigger pull, and while this doesn't mean the end of the world (unless maybe your gun is a .470 Nitro Express and you're facing an angry elephant), it's still a bit disconcerting. Many single triggers are of the inertia type; that is, it takes the recoil of the first shot to prepare the trigger to fire the second barrel. If for any reason the first shell misfires, you can't fire the second barrel unless you have presence of mind, and enough time, to work the selector switch (which nobody ever does). In this regard the double is no more reliable than an autoloader, which also is dependent upon perfect ammunition, and less so than a pump gun, with which you can manually eject the dud and load another shell by working the slide, a far more natural thing than trying to thumb a selector. Some single triggers are of the mechanical type, which means the second barrel can be fired simply by pulling the trigger again; no recoil is needed to prepare it for action.

Because the double gun has no long action to accommodate the shuffling in and out of shells which is typical of repeaters, it has a much shorter overall length. The advantages of a short gun in thick cover are obvious. It's easier to move with in the first place, less likely to collide with brush or limbs when swung, and so on. It has less total weight, and because it exerts less leverage out front, in effect concentrating the center of balance more between the hands than a longer gun, it's easier to get into action quickly. This is a plus when fast gun handling is called for, although on distant passing shots, where a regular swing-through is necessary, longer barrels with more weight out front will keep the gun moving smoothly and help prevent the sudden hesitation or "catch" which plagues many shooters who stop the gun to pull the trigger and shoot behind as a result. It's claimed that long barrels also make for more accurate pointing, for those who shoot that way, but this is debatable. The idea seems to make sense when a long-barreled gun is viewed from the side, but when seen from the rear, as in shooting, everything is drastically foreshortened and the apparent difference between 26-inch and 32-inch tubes is so insignificant it can be ignored.

It's possible to cut off the barrel of a pump or autoloader and add an adjustable choke, as I did with my Browning, in order to get a gun that's as short as practicable in the thickest brush. Probably some shot velocity is lost by this, but it's such an infinitesimal amount that it's unimportant, especially when compared with the enhanced handling qualities. With the barrel cut back and with the stock also slightly shortened, my "sweet sixteen" measures less overall than a 26-inch double gun. However, I've got to admit that such an operation does result in an odd-looking shotgun. The main problem is that down-bulging fore-end. Though necessary for enclosing essential autoloader parts and highly useful for proper gun control with the front hand, the result is that this bobtailed boomer has the profile of a pregnant dachshund. Nevertheless, I've never regretted the alteration, for the gun's efficiency was greatly improved. Still, there's no escaping the fact that much the same effect can be gained by selecting a good double; you then have all this shootability wrapped up in a handsome package. Assuming, of course, that you get a well-designed double, because some of the less craftsman-like doubles are dogs too.

Besides looks, the one unmatched quality of a double gun is that the two barrels give instant availability of different chokes. An adjustable unit like the Poly-Choke makes a repeater a versatile tool, but at any given time it actually offers but one choke to the hunter. He can choose his setting according to the cover and/or game, but once that is done he has committed himself. He just can't make a change after game is flushed. If he's in a thick corner with the unit cranked to improved cylinder and a pheasant put out by another hunter suddenly passes 45 yards away, he's out of luck. In such cases, the double gun user simply fires his tight barrel and probably takes home the bird. When a rooster is coming in to the hunter or going away (in either case the range is changing quickly) the single barrel shooter is stuck with whatever choke his gun has, while the double man picks the appropriate one for his first and second shots. (Years ago there *was* an adjustable choke which automatically tightened

Bob Bell's Ithaca SKB 12-ga. over/under has proved a top choice for pheasants, its improved cylinder and modified barrels handle most shots easily. But Ralph Cady, right, prefers his old slide-action Winchester.

with each shot, so you could start with improved cylinder, have a modified pattern for the second shot, and shoot a full choke for the third. This was an advantage on outgoing birds, a disadvantage on incomers. The unit was activated by the shot passing through. It could also be locked at a given choke. I understand that it has been discontinued now. I don't know whether it didn't work as well as hoped, whether there was not enough demand, or if it was too expensive to manufacture.)

At any rate, no one can deny the advantages of having an immediate choice of two chokes. The only problem in regard to this is the method by which the barrel to be fired first is selected. Two-trigger guns give a fast, easy choice. The front trigger normally fires the right (open) barrel, the rear trigger the left barrel. However, because the finger must have room to get between these two, it's obvious that the stock length is going to vary by approximately an inch, according to which trigger it's being measured from. A sixteenth of this distance is a vital measurement in the minds of many shotgunners (and sometimes rightly so), so it's not hard to understand why a single trigger is preferred by many. With such a unit, the same trigger fires both barrels, one at a time, so the gunner must have a means of deciding which barrel is to go first. A selector of some kind is the answer. In some models, such as the Browning Superposed and Winchester M101 over-under, the selector is integral with the tang safety. You move it left to select the open barrel (or right for the tight barrel), and then ahead to take the gun off safety. In other guns, such as the Ithaca SKB over/unders and the M21 Winchester side by side, the selector is a button in the top of the trigger, worked by the trigger finger. There may be men who in the fractured instant of shouldering the gun for a sudden flush can deliberately select one or the other barrel with one of these arrangements, but I've never met any of them. The normal procedure is to train yourself to thumb the selector for the open barrel first, as that's the one you'll want for the fast close flushes, and when it seems likely from the way the dog is working or whatever that the shot will be a long one, to choose the tight barrel by a conscious action. I've found it impracticable to work the selector of the SKB's with my trigger finger for field shots. One of these days I'm going to have a large flat head brazed onto that button so I can select the barrel while my finger is sliding inside the guard. Meanwhile its's simpler to just send the improved cylinder load at a far pheasant first—sometimes it does some good on its own—and slap off the modified barrel as quickly as possible. Remington's new M3200 over/under has a great advance in this area, the first significant change in barrel selectors in decades. Instead of requiring two distinct movements, left or right, then ahead, to select the firing barrel and get the safety off, simply pivoting the safety to one side or the other does both jobs at once.

I believe it was Val Browning who invented something called the "double-single" trigger, or something like that. If I understand it correctly, the idea was that you chose the open or tight barrel according to which trigger you pulled first (front for open, rear for choke), and then to fire the other barrel you simply pulled the same trigger again. This gave instant choke choice and did away with the necessity of moving the finger from one trigger to the other. There might be something to an idea like this, though I can't say it appeals to me personally. Actually, I'm not overly impressed with single triggers when the gun has two barrels. It's such a perfectly simple and satisfactory system to have one trigger for each barrel that I don't see any reason for trying to improve it. Fact is, I'm dubious that any single trigger selector arrangement, at least until the appearance of the M3200 Remington, has been a genuine improvement. It's easy to get your trigger finger to make a simple choice between a front and rear trigger. Trigger fingers are comparatively educated digits that react instinctively. Trying to remind your thumb to make some sort of squiggly movement in response to an instantaneous judgment of distance during the quarter-second it takes you to flip a gun to your shoulder, is, however, a bit much. Maybe you can do it. If so, congratulations. But I can't, and no one of my acquaintance can.

Everything considered, the easiest way I know to select instantly the firing order of a double gun's two barrels is through the use of two triggers. Single trigger fans like to make a big thing of the movement required to get from the front trigger to the rear one, often claiming it's necessary to slide the whole hand back (and therefore recommending a straight-grip stock). There are various reasons for preferring a straight grip, but it's not necessary to have one so double triggers can be used. I currently have six doubles: three over/unders and three side-by-sides. All of the former have single triggers and pistol grip stocks, and all of the latter have double triggers, with only one having a straight grip. I use them all regularly, handle them almost daily even when I can't pop a cap, and I know from experience that it's not necessary to shift the hand rearward when my finger moves from the front to the rear trigger, or forward when I reverse the firing order. And I also know that I can get off two shots with double triggers as fast as two with the single, at least when fired in the normal open-tight sequence. When you stop to think how a single trigger works, it's obvious that after firing the first shot the finger must relax its pressure, in effect reversing its direction of movement, then tighten again. On the double design, the finger presses the front trigger and continues its normal rearward movement, slipping off the side of the front trigger and immediately slapping the rear one. The reports from two shots fired this way almost blend. When the firing order is reversed, a little more time is necessary, for the finger has to move in the opposite direction after the first shot (as with the single trigger), and reach farther than is necessary with the single. For optimum results with twin triggers, the stock length must be precisely what's needed to let the finger just comfortably reach the front trigger with its end pad; if it extends farther across the trigger, you can't disengage without moving the hand or at least slackening the grip. But when the stock length is correct and the front trigger breaks, the trigger's slight rearward movement plus the normal reverse bend in the finger's first joint gives enough clearance so that the finger naturally continues back to hit the rear trigger. Obviously it would be simpler to determine an acceptable stock length if only one trigger had to be considered, but at the moment, so far as I'm concerned, double triggers have more to recommend them than singles. Perhaps the Remington 3200's easy-pivoting selector design will change my thinking, but I haven't yet had time to try it thoroughly in the field.

On most doubles, the thumb releases the safety, as it is located on top of the tang. It's equally convenient for a lefthander here, which is a point in its favor, but the often-repeated claim that it's faster than the cross-trigger safety of a pump or autoloader, which can be had for either right or lefthanders, is both debatable and pointless. When carrying a repeater, the forefinger normally lies across the guard, protecting the trigger from brush, etc. The rear joint of the finger is often in light contact with the head of the safety, or at least very close to it. When a bird flushes, a simple straightening, actually a stiffening, of the finger shoves the safety off. The base of the finger does it, not the tip, while the gun is being raised, and as the butt settles into the shoulder and the muzzle swings through the bird, the finger slaps the trigger. Timewise, I don't know how this compares to moving a tang safety off, but it has no importance because in either case the safety is disengaged in less time than it takes to shoulder the gun.

As with single triggers, automatic ejectors are another refinement of dubious worth on a double. There are times when their convenience is valuable, for they definitely save seconds in reloading. When the shooting is fast and furious something that's more likely on barn pigeons, where a lost bird is of no particular moment, than on ringnecks or grouse, they are great. For the reloader who saves his fired hulls they can be a nuisance, and in this day of nearly indestructible plastic cases, they can leave a highly visible trail through the countryside for years, a trail that antagonizes the landowner every time he sees it. Littering is littering, no matter whether it's empty cigarette packages or empty shotshells, and as a reloader who likes to get invited back to the same farms to hunt, I've found it worthwhile on two scores to take my empties home. It's no problem, actually, even with auto ejectors. After a normal shot or two, you simply cup one hand over the rear of the barrels as they've opened and catch the cases. Claybird shooters do it automatically. When more than a gunload of fast shots is needed, you bang them off and then retrieve the empties from the ground. It's easier to keep track of the cases from a double gun than a repeater, but it can be done with any.

As I've implied earlier, I like short barrels on shotguns. They handle better than long ones, get onto game quicker, and are easier to maneuver through thick cover. For decades the trend has been toward shorter barrels, but actual progress has been at the approximate speed of glaciers. Long barrels made some sense with muzzle-loaders. They got more efficiency from the black powder then in use, and the gun's length made it convenient to rest the butt on the ground with the barrel in the crook of the elbow while various reloading chores were performed. Black powder is long gone, so far as most of us are concerned, however, and we now do our loading from the breech end, yet many of those miserable long tubes are still with us. For what purpose nobody knows, although, admittedly, they swing smoothly for long, pointed-out shots such as some waterfowlers make, but on upland game any barrel longer than 26 inches is difficult for me to understand. I prefer less than a 26-inch barrel on a repeater, because of the long action, and I'd like to see 25-inch barrels offered on doubles.

It's true that short barrels have been offered by a few gun builders, and they did not sell well. However, some of these were just too expensive for most hunters, while others were not around long enough to gain a following. The fact is, few hunters actually give much thought to such matters. They assume the manufacturer knows best, and they buy what is offered. However, the manufacturer's main objective in life is to show a profit to his stockholders and one way this is done is by keeping inventory (such as a wide selection of barrel lengths) to a minimum. The average hunter's sheeplike acceptance of what's offered is also influenced by several well-known gunwriters who for many years have recommended 28- or 30-inch barrels on doubles and at least 26-inch barrels on repeaters. Now, these men are experts and in the proper context their comments are valid; however, they are based on their own experiences and the fact of the matter is, most of these gunners are over six feet in height. Barrels of the length they advise are for guns whose overall lengths are tailored to them. But anyone of short or medium height is handicapped with such lengths. It's not so much a matter of weight because a short broad man can be as strong as a tall slender one, but it is a question of handling qualities. Long barrels move the gun's center of balance forward, enough so that a shorter man, whose hands naturally are closer together than a tall man's when held in a similar attitude, cannot carry the gun in precisely the same way. Thus he cannot overcome its inertia and get it into action in the same way. Such things make a difference. A given gun is the same gun no matter who picks it up, but it will not—it can not—be handled exactly the same by any two persons, for no two are duplicates and they can't overcome that gun's inanimate resistance in the same way. Even if their heights and weights happen to be identical, their body conformations will differ, their muscles will have varying abilities, their reactions, their eyes, their nerves, even their thought processes will all be different. Each of these things has its effect.

Probably the best known exponent of short-barreled guns was the late Robert Churchill, a builder of high quality English doubles and an outstanding shooting coach. Churchill favored the 25-inch length and in his book, *Game Shooting,* presents excellent arguments for this length. What makes this particularly interesting is the fact that Churchill was of medium height and stocky build, lending support to the viewpoint that there is a direct relationship between the gunner's physical makeup and gun length. Common sense alone should suggest this, but apparently few persons consider it.

Many persons still believe that long-barreled guns shoot harder than short-barreled ones. There may have been some validity to this in black powder days (though even then it wasn't too significant in tubes of any practicable length), but velocity loss due to short barrels is unimportant when smokeless powders are used. It's common to find as much variation between shells out of the same box fired through a given barrel as will be lost by going from a 30-inch to a 26-inch length. On the average, a long barrel probably will give slightly higher velocity from a given load, but not enough to be important in the field and certainly not enough to make up for the comparative unhandiness of the longer gun.

Many hunters choose longer barrels to get the choke or choke combination they want. It's standard practice of American gunmakers to offer 26-inch barrels with improved cylinder boring (improved cylinder and modified in doubles), and 28- and 30-inch models in modified or full. This simplifies their inventories, but frustrates some hunters who have definite ideas about the combinations they'd like, such as modified and full in 26-inch length, but find they can't get them. Some high grade guns, and of course the custom jobs, can be obtained with any choke or combination of chokes. Most hunters probably don't give much thought to their gun's boring. How else can one explain the popularity of the full choke in the repeater and single shot for so long a period when modified or even improved cylinder is superior for most upland hunting? Still, some progress is being made, and it would come faster if a hunter could walk into a sporting goods store and choose from a more complete selection of chokes and barrel lengths.

The question of the best choice has be be faced. In a repeater to be used under average conditions, that is, in thick cover part of the time, in open fields and swales at other times, a modified choke is probably best. It isn't ideal at short or long range, but it is a good compromise. That, of course, is what it is intended to be. You sacrifice efficiency at either end of the range scale in order to best handle the greatest number of chances. It's possible to make a good argument for an improved cylinder choke in a single barrel gun for routine pheasant shooting; in fact, it's probably a better choice under most conditions than a full choke, because more birds are dropped at 25 yards than 50. I'd pick a full choke on a single barrel gun only if long experience in a given area had proved that the majority of shots were beyond 40 yards rather than under it. Few areas give such shooting. Probably the best solution to the question for the single barrel user is an adjustable choke such as the Cutts or Poly-Choke. The Cutts features tubes which are changed with a wrench, while the Poly is a collet type, instantly changed by a twist of the wrist. Some gunners have theorized that the Cutts design is more durable and possibly gives more regular patterns. I have no reliable data on this. I do know I have used a Poly-Choke for many years on my Browning autoloader and it's still performing flawlessly, and patterns I've shot with it show good distribution and densities that varied just as they should according to the setting.

For many experienced hunters, a pheasant gun is always a 12-ga. autoloader with long, full choke barrel, such as the M59 Winchester carried by John Plowman, standing, and Chick Holmes' Browning. But the author prefers a short-barreled double; ideally it would be choked improved cylinder and full, but this combination is hard to come by.

It isn't practical to fit double barrel guns with adjustable chokes. It sticks in my mind that I once saw a photograph of such an arrangement, so it might not be literally impossible, but so far as the average hunter is concerned, that's the situation. Of course, with two different chokes instantly available, a gunner has little need of any more. The trick is to get the combination which will best serve his shooting needs. Here is where things break down. It's been traditional in this country at least to offer doubles choked modified and full or improved cylinder and modified, the idea being to use the former for long range hunting, the latter for shorter shots. The trouble is, the modified and full combination is a handicap for thick cover hunting, and the improved cylinder and modified doesn't cut it at the long distances. Everything considered, the best choke combination for average bird hunting has to be the improved cylinder/full. I don't know of any American-made shotgun that's routinely offered with these borings, yet it's obvious that given your choice of two of the three standard chokes, the modified is the least useful, no matter how desirable it is in a single barrel gun. It's the addition of the second barrel that eliminates the need for the modified choke. An improved cylinder barrel will handle all shots up to 35 yards or so. On shots longer than 35 yards the full choke is more practical. The outer limit of the improved cylinder barrel and the nearer distances at which the full choke would normally be used overlap the modified's

What to Hit Him With . . . the Gun 131

range bracket so completely that there is no true need for this compromise boring in a double. I'd like to see the standard hunting double made with 26-inch barrels bored improved cylinder and full, with the variations from this being the special order items, rather than the reverse situation as now exists (assuming you can get an improved cylinder and full boring even on special order). It would serve the needs of most gunners far better than today's standard choices.

Two other approaches to the choke question are available. First, just as the introduction of the plastic shotcup/wad tightened the patterns delivered by a given gun, special shells called "brush" or "scatter" loads can be used when more open patterns than a barrel normally gives are wanted. These usually feature cardboard dividers within the shot charge; either a couple of flat round ones that divide the shot into three layers or an "X" affair that is installed so that if viewed from the front end the charge is divided into quadrants. The effect of these wads is to spread the pellets more than usual shortly after they leave the muzzle, so that a modified or full choke barrel can be used for brush hunting. My experience with them is limited. They seem to work fairly well, though it's not likely they will give patterns as evenly distributed as a conventional shell in an improved cylinder bore. Handloaders can get a similar, and possibly superior, effect by using cube or flattened shot, rather than the normal spherical type.

Another possible way of opening patterns is to use standard length shells in magnum length chambers. Testing by some gunners indicates that shooting 2¾" shells in a 3" chamber opens patterns about one full degree of choke. This is only an approximation as performance varies with the particular load and gun, but if it works, it's a handy gimmick for it can make the average modified-choke repeater, which is a fine choice for most pheasant hunting, into an improved-cylinder outfit for use in tight cover.

Don't ever reverse this procedure and try to use 3" Magnum shells in a 2¾" chamber. They'll fire, of course, but those long cases won't have room for the crimp to completely unfold within the enlarged chamber area. The front of the case will extend into the forcing cone (that inner section of the barrel where the chamber diameter tapers down to bore diameter), and the shot charge/wad will have to force its way through a considerably undersize hole. This boosts pressures and adversely affects patterns. Personally, though, I think it would be simpler for everyone if we could just get short-barreled, improved cylinder/full doubles in our local sporting goods stores.

A raised rib helps many shooters hit targets, I believe. There's no doubt about this in trap shooting, where most competitors actually aim at a claybird much as they would with a rifle. The flat, sharp-cornered top of the rib, which is matted or filed to reduce glare, makes for easy alignment with an already-shouldered gun, and any good trap shooter knows precisely where the trailing corner of his rib was in relation to a crossing bird when he fired. I have a hunch that most good skeet shooters know this almost as well as their trap-shooting cousins, despite the fact that this game was designed to simulate hunting conditions. The rib has a further quality important to a claybirder: it helps dissipate the heat waves which rise from the barrel after several fast shots and distort his view of the target.

Shotgun hunters rarely have to worry about heated barrels, although it's a problem they'd like to have more often, yet I still think a rib helps. Many gunners like to say they never see the barrel or the front sight when they shoot at game, and I've no doubt they believe this. The bird, of course, is and should be the focus of attention. Nevertheless, when a shooter's cheek is pressed against the stock and he's gazing down along the top of that barrel, there's no way in the world to keep it from registering on his awareness to some extent. The field of view of his eyes, even when narrowed in concentration on the target, is not so small that he literally sees nothing else. That barrel and sight are in there somewhere toward the bottom edge: indistinct, fuzzy, probably only about the forward half or one-third registering and that possibly only subconsciously; nevertheless, the front end of the gun is there, and I've a notion that a flat-top, non-reflecting rib is a bit more conspicuous or definable than the rounded, "wavy," light-reflecting top of a single-barrel gun. If that be the case, the shooter undoubtedly has a tendency to shift the gun into proper relationship with the target when he senses the two are out of alignment, even if his gaze isn't actually focusing on the rib, sight, or any other part of the gun, and even if he isn't fully aware of the correction he's making. He doesn't necessarily do this on every chance. Some are pure "reaction" shots: just *flush-bang!* But the speed with which a shot is taken is often influenced by the bird itself. A bird which is going to vanish in an instant brings an extremely fast shot, while one that will be in range for several seconds tends to slow the gunner down. In the latter case, he uses all the time available to get the best gun alignment possible, and on such chances, even if he doesn't realize it, the rib is a help.

This is not necessarily the best way of shooting. Many top gunners take all their shots at the same speed, or as close to it as the somewhat imperfect reactions of even gifted humans allow, preferring to plaster an occasional close bird rather than foul up their normal timing. A few of these are so good they center their small, close-range patterns on the head and neck of a rooster and therefore aren't concerned with either rhythm problems or shot-up birds. But such shooting takes a perfectly fitted gun plus great skill. Most hunters are not in the class of these experts, and it's normal to take advantage of anything which seems likely to increase their chances of a hit, such as an extra second or so for gun alignment. Here again the rib helps. The top game gunner has less need for a rib than a so-so shooter, because he's going to hit the vast majority of birds regardless, yet he's the one who is most likely to have this appurtenance because, among other things, he likes guns and a rib creates a nice visual effect, giving a finished look to a barrel. The less interested gunner tends not to have one because it costs extra. He can buy what seems like a lot of shells, or beer, for the price of that skinny piece of steel.

Some raised ribs are ventilated, meaning the top rests on a series of tiny legs with narrow openings between, while others are solid. Theoretically, the latter are better for hunting guns, as they can't collect seeds, bits of weeds, or whatever as the ventilated rib sometimes does, and they offer fewer half-hidden surfaces where rusting might begin. In practice, there's little difference; a moment's work with an oil-soaked "Q-Tip" banishes the problems.

Some trap guns have unusually wide ribs, but these aren't normal to field guns, and there's even some question about their value at trap. Occasionally other questions come up about ribs: how high they should be above the barrel; whether they should be flat or slightly concave; whether they should be parallel to the center of the

Al Bachman uses his restocked Winchester 21 with a ventilated rib for most everything that flies or runs. Bell's M21 is a 20-ga. bored modified and full. With this combination the author once accounted for twenty-one kills with twenty-two shots at ringnecks.

bore or at a slight angle; whether their width should be constant from end to end or taper so that the lines of the edges, if extended, seem to meet at some particular distance. Even the method used to insure a non-reflecting surface is debated at times. Those interested in such details can argue endlessly, but so far as the average hunter is concerned they're unimportant.

To the shooter, a rib's appearance on an over/under is about the same as on a repeater, but it is not exactly the same, at least to my eyes, because of the different overall conformation of the guns and the somewhat different shooting styles they require. Nevertheless, as seen from above, an over/under appears to have only one barrel and repeaters and single-shots in actuality have but one. By comparison, a side-by-side double presents a wide obtrusion in the lower portion of the shooter's field of view, so wide that many trap shooters say one reason they do not use side-by-sides is that the broad muzzle makes it too difficult for them to know precisely where they are holding in relation to the bird. This is rarely if ever a problem on gamebirds, and I've a hunch that a wide front end, subconsciously seen, is a benefit for field shooting. If my memory is correct, the late Bob Nichols, when gun editor of *Field and Stream,* designed an item called the "Bev'l Blok," which was a sort of conspicuous ramp for the front sight on a repeater, intended to serve as an eye-catcher during fast shooting. I believe this grew out of the practice of some shooters of

What to Hit Him With . . . the Gun   135

wrapping a wide strip of adhesive tape around the muzzle. An adjustable choke, which is usually larger in diameter than barrel, serves the same function. These all point up the fact that many shooters in one way or another recognize that it's often a distinct help to be able to visually relate their gun muzzles to the target.

Even though the side-by-side's wide muzzles in themselves are eye-catchers, and the twin tubes provide a different visual effect than a single-barrel—the shadow that divides unribbed barrels sometimes makes a "sight" for the person who shoots deliberately, whereas an unribbed single barrel often presents only a glare to the gunner's eyes—it's common to fit doubles with raised ribs. These come in various configurations too. On my Winchester 21, the slightly concave rib is flush with the top of the frame at the back end and, due to the decreasing diameter of the barrels beyond the chambers, is higher than the barrels are in the central portion of their length, but the rib winds up even with the top of the muzzles. In other words, it slants downhill noticeably. By comparison, the flat rib on Dad's old L. C. Smith begins even higher at the rear where the action bulges slightly to accept the top extension, then rides well above the barrels all the way to wind up almost 3/16" above the tops of the muzzles, so high that when shot normally the visual effect is almost the same as is given by a single-barrel gun. Nevertheless, both systems work, that is, they put their patterns where expected, because their stocks vary considerably. The Winchester, which has been restocked, has a high thick comb, while the Smith has more drop at the comb and is narrower in cross section where the face contacts the stock. If nothing else, this indicates that any rib type can work well if it is integrated into the overall design of the individual gun, and that gun fits the user at least reasonably well.

Sights on a shotgun are another debatable item. All have at least a front bead when new—it isn't uncommon for these to be knocked off by brush or to fall off for whatever reason, and their absence often goes unnoticed—and many have a smaller bead somewhat ahead of the midpoint of the barrel, the intention probably being to help gun alignment. There isn't much practical value in such an arrangement for game shooting, as very few shots are actually aimed and aiming is the basic purpose of a sight. Because of their small size, front sights are much less conspicuous than the gun muzzle itself, and, as has been noted earlier, even the muzzles are often seen only subconsciously. So when we get away from the more or less grooved targets of the claybird ranges, shotgun sights lose importance. Still, they can have some merit, particularly the two-bead setup. Even if not usable for fast-flushing game, they often indicate very closely if comb height and thickness are what they should be. If the shooter shoulders a new gun normally, cheeking it as he would to fire at a moving target, and the rear bead seems to touch or nestle slightly into the bottom of the front one, forming a sort of figure eight, it's likely that the stock comb is about right. This isn't a positive check. It takes test firing under controlled conditions to determine precisely where patterns go, but quite often shooting proves it to be accurate. It also often shows up gross errors in stock fit, such as in a poor restocking job or a factory stock that's way too long or too short. If a definite change in head position is necessary to properly align the two beads when the gun is shouldered rapidly as in hunting, there's almost bound to be something wrong with the fit.

Stock dimensions are critically important on a shotgun if top results are demanded. It's possible to achieve a good level of field performance with a stock that fits only passably well, or even what seem to be excellent results when judged against the ability of the average hunter, who isn't really too hot a performer. A top shot will hit the majority of his targets with any gun, once he's had the chance to fire a few shells to learn where it's putting its loads, but he has to work at it far more with a poorly fitting stock than he would with a properly fitting one. He hits in spite of the stock, not because of it. However, extremely high levels of shooting on a day-after-day, week-after-week level are attained only by a very skillful shooter using a gun that fits him in all details.

It would be nice if we could all have custom-tailored stocks built to our precise needs by best-quality gunmakers. Doubtless our shooting proficiency would improve noticeably. However, this isn't possible, so most of us have to make do with factory issue designs or whatever the result is after we cobble these up a bit. The truth is, these conditions can produce reasonably successful guns. It's become a sort of fad for gunwriters to look down their noses at factory stocks, implying if not stating outright that they can't see how anyone can ever hit a bird with one of these New England-handled smoothbores. I haven't the slightest doubt, however, that 99.9999% of all birds taken in this country are dropped with as-issue guns. This is not to suggest that many, and perhaps a great majority, of these shooters would not do better with stocks whittled to their precise specifications and adapted to their shooting habits, but the fact still remains that they do get birds. As with the experts, if to a lesser degree, they, too, overcome their stocks' deficiencies and "make do." And there's an outside chance that they don't even have to overcome as much as some suspect. Those guys at Remington, Winchester, Ithaca, Savage, and elsewhere just might be a bit brighter than a lot of writers give them credit for; they could well be building stocks of "average" dimensions for the simple reason that there are a helluva lot of "average dimension" shooters out there.

Unfortunately, I don't happen to be one of them, and maybe you aren't either. After more than a few years of fooling around with shooting irons I've come to recognize that almost always the only thing I have to do to make a scattergun fit me reasonably well is shorten the stock. And several friends who happen to be considerably taller than I am tell me that the only alteration they regularly make to a factory stock is to lengthen it. I point this out because there have been millions of words written about stock fit. Every dimension, line, angle, thickness, or whatever has been examined from every possible viewpoint. All this makes interesting reading, and some of the conclusions are even valid. Most of the time, however, a hunter will find that if he gets the stock length and comb height right, he has a gun that fits pretty well. It will not necessarily be perfect, understand, but it will fit well enough that he can become a very good field shot with it. If he wants to become an outstanding shot, chances are he'll have to go to a full custom model, but here's something most gunwriters never mention, perhaps because the thought never went through their little pointed noggins. Not one hunter out of 10,000 has the slightest desire to be a truly great shotgunner! I admit this sounds like heresy, but all the average hunter wants to do is hit a reasonable number of the birds he shoots at. He isn't tormented by that inner demon that drives the few well-known shooters. His missed birds are soon forgotten; they never even come back to haunt his dreams, difficult as that may be for the gun scribblers to understand. Fact is, many guys I know are so little bothered by misses that they rarely remember they've ever made any! And I'm not sure that's a bad way to be. . . .

If it happens, however, that someone you know isn't hitting as many birds as he'd like to and the thoughts of a new gun or a new stock are going through his mind, it might pay for him to experiment with the current one a bit before investing a considerable amount of money. The two stock dimensions mentioned earlier, length of pull and comb height, have an awful lot to do with gun fit. Fortunately, it isn't hard to determine if one or both should be changed, they are easy to alter if necessary, and the expense is slight.

Length is the first thing to consider. You have to be able to get the gun to your shoulder before any other dimension becomes operative. There's no use meddling with something else first and then finding that it has to be changed again after the length is altered. Technically, stock length is the distance in inches from the point where your finger presses the trigger to the center of the buttplate. From a shooting standpoint, you don't give a hoot what this measurement is, you just know what you have to be able to shoulder the gun quickly, swing it smoothly in any direction and fire comfortably. What this means is that the stock must be short enough to slide up to its pocket inside your shoulder muscle without dragging on whatever clothes you happen to be wearing (and it should be remembered that these vary with the season, species of game hunted, etc.), and long enough that when the shot is made the nose of the comb keeps your recoiling thumb away from your nose. When the stock is functional in these respects, the length is okay. There's no big mystery about the thing, no magic formula for determining length; you just want something that works.

A stock that's too long leads to bad shooting habits, probably worse ones than a too-short stock. As a fella who grew up shooting over-lengthy items, I can vouch for this. In order to shoulder one of those monstrosities (I never knew anyone back then with the temerity to cut one off; after all, if the factory made it that length, that *had* to be the correct one!), I got in the habit of swinging my body around so I was facing away at a good angle from the direction I intended to shoot, much as the army used to teach riflemen to stand in the offhand position. That made it possible to mount a too-long stock. And the gun was handled in a much the same, across-the-chest, GI manner. Fact is, I still tend to operate from this position —old habits are hard to overcome—but it's better if the target can be faced more squarely. You then can swing well in either direction, rather than just one.

When you're certain that a stock is too long, you shorten it. If it has a recoil pad, remove it and do some shooting with the butt bare. Chances are, it will be a bit too short now, but if it happens to be just right, you simply have the stock cut off an amount equal to the thickness of the pad, following the original angle of pitch, and have the pad reinstalled. Unless you're a good woodworker, this should be done by a professional, for it's not nearly as simple a job as it seems. It's difficult to get a clean, non-splintery cutoff, and even harder to work the pad down to its new size without ruining the stock finish. It helps to wrap masking tape around the rear of the stock before the cut is made and while grinding down the pad, but this is not complete protection. A careful workman can do an acceptable job, though. Make certain that the top and bottom lines of the pad continue those of the stock, rather than angling off in some weird direction as many do. After awhile it'll give you the galloping mugwumps to look at a goof like that. If the original stock has no recoil pad, remove the buttplate and slice off a bit at a time, doing considerable shooting after each cut. When you find the proper length, take your gun to a guy who knows how and tell him to install a recoil pad to that overall length. He'll remove your last amateur cut to put on the pad, and you'll have a properly fitting stock, at least insofar as length goes.

Factory stocks tend to have plenty of length for the average-size gunner. For the few tall, long-armed persons who need a longer one, the addition of a recoil pad of proper thickness is usually enough. Pads come in various thicknesses, so it's not difficult to get just what's needed. The minute percentage of shooters which needs more length than the pad can give must resort to a filler block beneath the pad or a completely new stock.

Comb height is the other important dimension, for it largely governs where your pattern will hit in the vertical plane. The only way you can tell with certainty where it's hitting now is by shooting. Put up a large sheet of paper (Sometimes you can get a newspaper printer to give you the tag end of a roll of newsprint, pieces of which

Jim Bashline and his beautiful old Ithaca. Restocked to his dimensions and with wide open tubes, it handles all close-to-medium shots perfectly. Bell again is using his Ithaca SKB.

work well when thumb-tacked against a piece of celotex or whatever.), with an eight-inch aiming point in the middle. From a range of perhaps 25 yards, rapidly shoulder the gun as when firing at a live target. (Because you don't have time to aim when hunting, you don't test in that way either.) Your eyes should be focused on the aiming point, and once they are and the gun is up, shoot. If a number of patterns consistently go to about the same place, no matter where it is, you are shooting okay. If they cover the aiming point, preferably with the center of the pattern a bit high, no more need be done. The gun is essentially shooting where you're looking, with a built-in allowance for the flushing-bird shots that are normal in American upland hunting. Having a gun put about two-thirds of its pattern above the level of the muzzle at normal ranges also permits the shooter to keep the bird in view just above the muzzles when swinging on a passing shot, an arrangement liked by many.

If the patterns don't go where you're looking, you've got to zero in. Almost all riflemen know they must do this occasionally, but few shotgunners give it much thought, either because they assume all shotguns shoot precisely where they look, or because they believe the pattern's size will take care of any slight error. These are poor assumptions, often leading to scratch hits or outright misses. Many single-barrel guns do not put their patterns where you expect, and many doubles throw their two patterns to two different places. They're supposed to coincide at 40 yards and most of the time these will overlap to some extent at that distance, but it's fairly unusual for the centers of both patterns to hit the same point. It's common to have one higher or lower or off to one side or the other. High-grade guns tend to approach the ideal more than inexpensive ones (such regulation is part of the reason why doubles are comparatively expensive); nevertheless, there are thousand-dollar guns around which don't center patterns at the same place.

If the impacts of a double are noticeably far apart at the conventional 40 yards, there isn't anything the average gunner can do to correct it. Sometimes changing loads will help. The better guns are often adjusted with a particular load, either to the buyer's specifications for a custom gun or to handle the class of loads normal for whatever type of game will usually be hunted: upland birds with a 26" improved cylinder and modified gun, waterfowl with a 30" modified and full, etc. Sometimes nothing can be done, short of disassembling the tubes and completely reworking their joining.

Even custom-built guns do not always shoot to the point expected, for in addition to such mechanical problems as allowing for the recoil effect which is working on the gun long before the shot leaves the muzzle and which comes rearward in a different line from each barrel, trying to rotate the gun in a horizontal plane around the fulcrum of the stock on the shoulder and in the same short time period moving in other directions in response to various forces and resistances, differences in pattern placement also result from differences in gun handling. What was fine for the gun builder's test shooter may be so-so for the ultimate owner, because different people have different ways of absorbing recoil, their hand grips are different, the surface of the shoulder where the butt makes contact may be different, and the way the face presses against the side and comb of the stock is different. The chances are good these two persons even see things differently. All of these things, and more, have certain effects on a pattern's location. Furthermore, the hunter's habit of using two different types of loads in a double, say a field load of 7½s in the open barrel and a magnum load of 6s or 4s in the tight one, can cause problems. The recoil effect of the heavy load and the different time period for its charge to clear the barrel can in themselves be enough to send the second shot to a different place than the first. And there's no way of knowing things like this except by test firing the exact loads you're going to use on some sort of pattern board at a measured distance. If, despite all your testing, changing loads, etc., a double's barrels continue to shoot to different places, you've got a real problem. Even if one barrel hits where you want it, the better you point the other one the farther you'll miss. If it's a high-grade piece on which the manufacturer has built a reputation, it might be possible he'll re-regulate it, but if it's an inexpensive or mediocre job probably the smartest thing to do is to get rid of it.

If a double throws both its loads to essentially the same point, yet that point is not where you're looking when you gaze out along that super-efficient rib that was supposed to solve all your hitting problems, or that old long-barreled auto simply doesn't shoot where it seems to be looking, you can probably put things all together by working on the stock. Usually it's the comb's height or thickness that makes the difference here. A shotgun has no rear sight that can be zeroed in like a rifle's—and there's rarely enough time to use one if it existed—so the comb serves this function. The gunner's face, hopefully pressed against the stock the same for every shot, aligns the eye above the rib with more than enough accuracy for the job. When the comb height is correct for the configuration of the shooter's face and his gun handling habits, the pattern travels along a projection of his gaze. If the comb is too high, or sometimes too thick as that has a similar effect, the pattern goes high. A low comb gives low shot placement. When serious testing indicates one of these faults exists, comb height can be reduced with sandpaper—slowly, with a good amount of test shooting at every stage. The low comb can be raised temporarily with moleskin or other thin stick-on material. When patterns consistently hit where you want them in relation to the muzzle, and they do this when the gun is handled rapidly and without deliberate aiming, as in actual hunting, that's it. A sanded-down stock can now be refinished, a built-up one will have to have permanent material installed to duplicate the additions, or a completely new stock may be fashioned to the new dimensions. Regardless, the improved handling quality and hitting characteristics will more than pay for the work and cost.

As indicated earlier, getting the length of pull and the comb height correct will in themselves usually give good field results, but obviously any further improvement in stock fit will also bring some benefit. We don't have the space to go into such material here, and there's no good reason to do it because so much good data is already available. Anyone looking for a book on the subject might read Robert Arthur's *The Shotgun Stock,* published by A. S. Barnes and Co., Inc., Cranbury, New Jersey 08512. There may be other books on shotgun stocks, but I've never seen a better one.

Shotgun fore-ends are not nearly as much of a problem as their stocks. In fact, one hunter I know has completely removed the fore-end from an autoloader just to save the weight. (He's a grouse hunter, incidentally.) Fore-ends serve various functions in the different gun designs, but so far as the hunter is concerned they're simply a handle to hang onto with the forward hand, or, in the case of pump guns, the unit that also makes it possible to fire repeated shots. Pumps, autoloaders, and over/unders by their inherent design have hand-filling fore-ends, and this is an advantage for it gives the shooter more control over his gun. The oldstyle "splinter" fore-end found on many American and most English side-by-sides is useless as a handgrip, but most of the time this isn't important because the shooter usually grasps the barrels as well, his thumb and fingers bracketing them while that tiny wood sliver nests in his palm. This is okay when the shots are infrequent, but if they're coming so fast that the barrels get hot, it's obviously impractical. The English get around this by use of a leather-covered handguard that slides over the barrels from the muzzle end and protects the hand. It's split on top to leave the rib and sights uncovered. Undoubtedly this works all right, but it seems an odd contraption with which to doctor up a $4,000 Purdey. Far more suitable, I feel, is a conventional beavertail fore-end as developed in this country. I say "conventional" because, as with many other things, some stock whittlers obviously feel that if a little added wood is a good thing, a lot is better. Some of the beavertails they've created would make enough fuel to keep a New England fireplace hot from Christmas to New Year's. Such monstrosities don't add a thing to a gun's handling qualities, they're unnecessarily heavy, and in addition they look like hell. All that's needed in a beavertail is enough width and length to keep the fingers from unexpectedly grasping a hot barrel. The depth should be no greater than the action at the rear end, although it won't angle upward toward the front as radically as the splinter job. Ideally, it will taper to a slightly wider dimension at the front than at the action, so that recoil tends to tighten it in the shooter's grasp, rather than loosen it as a conventional taper does.

Trigger pull is not as touchy a matter on shotguns as it is on rifles, which is just as well as it's a lot harder to adjust on a smoothbore than on a varmint gun. Few shotgunners will quibble with the pull on a good repeater such as the Remington 870, Ithaca 37, Winchester 12, and similar models, but a few of the more advanced gunners get picky about the twin triggers on doubles, preferring somewhat different weights of pull to compensate for the different leverages offered by these, and so on. These arguments are valid for the expert shot, but I'm dubious as to whether they make much difference to the fellow who wants only to kill a few birds a year. So long as his triggers are fairly crisp—and this isn't always the case even with expensive guns—preferably with weights of around four pounds, they'll do.

Safeties are standard items on all hunting guns. (Some guns intended only for claybird shooting don't have them and others have arrangements whereby they can be made inoperative.) My only comment on safeties is that they should always be used but never trusted. The reason is simple. In practically all shotguns, the safety works only on the trigger. Opening a double or working the action of a repeater to chamber a shell automatically cocks the gun. When the action is closed, you have a cocked and loaded firearm in your hands, in other words, a gun that's ready to shoot. Putting the safety "on" makes it safer than it was, but it isn't truly safe. It's never safe in the sense that a military rifle, such as the M1903 Springfield, is when its safety is on. The Springfield's safety securely locks the firing pin, a solid ridge of metal prevents it from dropping no matter how the rifle is handled. However, in the vast majority of shotguns putting the safety on merely moves a metal bar into a position that, at best, prevents the trigger from moving when pressed. The tumbler (internal hammer; there's one for each barrel) is not locked back in any way except by its regular notch in the trigger/sear/tumbler linkup. This notch can get worn in an old gun, or may not even fit well in a new one. It is quite possible for a sudden blow, as from a dropped gun, to jar these pieces out of their proper relationship. In such a case, the compressed mainspring slams the tumbler forward, striking the shell's primer, and the gun fires. Some gun designs have an intercepting unit that's supposed to catch the falling tumbler and many times it probably does. Other times, the jar that disengages the original contact also puts the interceptor out of action. So it is possible to have a gun fire even when the safety is in "on" position. Where it will send its load of shot depends, as always, on precisely where the muzzle is pointing. If you've made it an absolute habit never to let that muzzle point at anything you wouldn't want to hit, there's no problem other than embarrassment if it does go off unexpectedly. Otherwise, you can kill your hunting buddy! So use that safety to take advantage of the times it does work, but don't trust it, ever.

Some double guns have automatic safeties; that is, breaking the action to reload moves the safety on automatically. Before the gun can be fired, the safety must be manually moved to the "off" position. I suppose this is intended to make it unnecessary for the gunner to remember to put the gun on safe after shooting, but I don't like the arrangement. A hunter soon forms the habit of putting the safety on when he wants it on, but when a series of fast shots is necessary, as on passing doves, called crows, or even on rare occasions at pheasants, an automatic safety is a real nuisance. Maybe this is a personal feeling resulting from the fact that only one of my guns has this device, which keeps me from becoming truly familiar with it, but I can't see that anything important is gained through its use, and it causes lost shots for me.

8

How to Hit Him

Making a killing shot on pheasants, as indicated earlier, can be quite difficult . They're big, tough birds. Hitting them, though, should be fairly easy because their size and their takeoff characteristics make them a comparatively easy target. Yet an awful lot of ringnecks are missed cleanly, and far too many are hit badly and dropped as cripples, which is even worse, for a running rooster is close to impossible to recover without a good dog. I doubt if any other gamebird suffers as high a percentage of lost cripples. As a result, shooting skill becomes important.

A reasonable degree of shooting talent should be an obvious requirement for anyone who hunts, and yet the vast majority of license buyers do not pick up a gun, let alone fire one, from one season to the next. They seem to believe that their frontier background—after all, most Americans feel they're only a few generations removed from Daniel Boone and Davy Crockett—is all that's necessary for them to maintain the true gunman's ability. This of course is ridiculous. Shooting well is as difficult, perhaps more so, as playing golf or tennis well, yet no one would think he could maintain a high level of proficiency at these sports without regular practice. Yet, countless hunters apparently believe that buying a box of shells

Sometimes it's just BANG-BANG, and two birds hanging dead in the air.

and grabbing a gun is all the preparation needed for hitting birds. Such hunters get some birds, but they cripple and lose more than they get, and they miss more than they cripple. At best, this is a miserable state of affairs; at worst, it's a horrible waste. No one who thinks of himself as a sportsman would condone such sloppiness with instruments of the hunt.

The basic purpose of hunting is to obtain meat. To do this, one kills. There's no other way possible on this earth. Sport hunting is as legitimate a means to this end as anything else; as reasonable as raising a steer to be slaughtered and sold in the supermarket, say. In my opinion it is more so, for the hunter is directly involved. He knows what he is doing, and he takes responsibility for his acts, rather than hiding behind the numerous layers of today's table of organization, the breeder, rancher, transporter, jobber, dealer, slaughterer, distributor, meat cutter, checkout clerk, which for most of our population intervenes between a living animal and a Saran-wrapped piece of meat. Nevertheless, the hunter's willingness to kill and accept the responsibility of killing is not enough. Due to his very involvement with the animal, if nothing else, he owes it a clean, quick death. Because the tool he uses for this act is a gun, he has the obligation of acquiring a reasonable skill with it. No man reaches perfection with guns (or with anything else, not even the slaughterer's sledgehammer), but he should make a genuine effort in that direction.

Just as one acquires skill at golf or tennis by playing golf or tennis, one gets good at shooting by shooting. That's only logical, yet an awful lot of hunters avoid pre-season shooting and gun handling. This is hard for me to understand. If it is at all possible, I think each hunter should be out somewhere shooting at least once a week. My wife says I have to shoot something every day to be happy, which is an exaggeration, of course . . . but not much. Just to handle a gun, flipping it to my shoulder to center a door knob or swinging it along the ceiling-wall joint from corner to corner, gives me pleasure. Lordy me, just looking at a rack full of nice guns makes me feel good. To be able to shoot them daily, if only a round of trap or skeet or at a few barn pigeons, say, would make this old world something like the Happy Hunting Grounds for me. So I can't understand why so many hunters don't shoot more. Anyone who enjoys hunting must have some feeling for guns, so the shooting itself should be pleasurable, and it would make his field results a lot more satisfying.

I realize that a lot more shooting would be done if it were more convenient to do it, and if it didn't cost so much. Not everyone lives where he can step out his back door and go hunting, or even within a quarter-hour's drive of a claybird range. And the price of shells is something we all have to consider. Yet a little honest effort can make a hunter a better game shot—even without popping a cap. If we add to this the nominal cost of a few rounds of trap or skeet at a local range, or a case of clay pigeons thrown with a hand trap, an average hunter will be far better prepared for the opening day of the season than is otherwise possible. Obviously, for the hunter who isn't a year-round shooter, the time to practice is just before the season opening. The first day is the one that offers the most and the easiest shots. To flub these (in effect, practicing on the live birds), is a ridiculous approach. Yet far too many hunters work this way.

Shooting is like anything else in the sense that there's a right way and a wrong way to do it. An old aphorism says "A blind hog gets an acorn once in awhile," and it's equally true that a poor shot hits a pheasant now and again. But a good shot hits most of the pheasants he shoots at, and an expert shot hits (and kills) almost all of them. A serious hunter who takes pride in his gunning ability and works at it a bit reaches the point where he's genuinely surprised when a bird doesn't drop when he shoots. When he doesn't feel this way it's because he realizes, even as he shoots, that he's taking a shot he should pass up. Many times birds pass far out of range and anyone but the true beginner knows he should not take a shot. There are numerous other shots, however, which are almost—but not quite—within sure killing range, and it takes quite a bit of experience to recognize this fact and restrain yourself from touching off a shot. This is further complicated by the fact that if enough such chances are taken, some will be instant kills. These lucky hits will lead the unthinking to believe such shots are acceptable chances and to feel that as his skill increases they will become routine. Yet the experienced hunter knows that only luck directed a single pellet into the brain, and that for every clean kill at that distance perhaps a dozen birds will be hit in the body with a pellet or two and be wasted insofar as the hunter is concerned. We simply don't have enough game birds

With one ringneck falling to Bell's gun—Sam's gaze riveted to it—Bashline swings on a second that was outside of the camera's field.

that we can afford to treat them like this. Nationwide, the average pheasant kill is less than one bird per licensed hunter per season. Even allowing for the considerable sections of the country where ringnecks are not found but hunters are, this is enough to prove we can't tolerate sloppy shooting.

How does a hunter learn to shoot well, or at least well enough? By practice. There's no shortcut. You simply have to handle a gun often enough and consistently enough so that it looks where you're looking and you're looking in the right place. The better a gun fits, the easier this is to do, but a perfectly fitting gun will not, by itself, kill birds. The gunner is the ultimate controlling factor. He decides whether a particular shot will be tried, precisely when it will be fired, and how. Sometimes it seems otherwise. A flushing bird is dropped so quickly and easily that to an inexperienced onlooker the whole thing seems akin to magic. The truth is, however, everything clicks so perfectly because this kind of a shooter has trained himself to react in a certain way to a certain stimulus. Instead of waiting until he has flushed a bird to learn how to swing-mount-shoot, he has prepared for this moment by going through his shooting procedures thousands, or more likely tens of thousands, of times previously. He rarely fires a shot during these procedures. It isn't necessary in the first place, and because this practicing is done indoors, it is impossible. It doesn't take long, perhaps ten minutes a day, but this is time enjoyably spent, because such a man loves the sight and feel and movement of guns to begin with. He gains pleasure from handling them, and, of course, it's profitable because he learns to hit well. Even these few minutes add up, for in this daily period a man can go through his gun mounting drill fifty times, and this adds up to well over 10,000 times per year. This alone does wonders for a hunter's ability, because the daily contact makes his gun a perfectly familiar thing, almost a living extension of himself, rather than the strange-feeling chunk of wood and steel that it seems to the one-week-a-year shooter.

Gun handling also keeps the necessary muscles toned up so they can easily handle their chores. If a 6- or 7-pound gun is raised from hip to shoulder level, swung, and lowered again fifty times or so in a ten-minute period, a reasonable amount of muscular energy is expended. Furthermore, a conditioned response is set up. You're standing there, the gun in normal carrying position, and something says "go." Eyes focused on the bird—which may be the three-way intersection of two walls with the bedroom ceiling—the feet move into position, the gun flows upward, safety coming off as it rises, the hands automatically tightening to prevent bounce and absorb recoil as the butt seats itself in the shoulder, the finger slaps the front trigger just as the dimly seen muzzle moves through the "bird," and slides back to hit the rear trigger as the muzzle continues to swing out along the wall-ceiling jointure. Sometimes the swing is to the right, sometimes to the left, sometimes up or down, depending on how the gunner "sees" his birds. That's no matter. The basic drill is the same, and the gunner is gaining proficiency with every swing.

When the procedure has been carried out often enough, it becomes automatic, just like the oldtime gunfighter's conditioned response. This occasionally leads to a problem in the field. The sound of a flushing bird is often the stimulus that activates this response. A good percentage of the time, that bird is going to be a hen, a critter that's normally protected. The hunter who has brought himself to this level of response is quite likely swinging on the bird, tracking the sound of its flush or the blur of its movement, before he fully recognizes what it is. If it's a protected sex or species, he has only a fractured second to abort the shot. Sometimes he fails at this, as Bill Hickok once failed when he whirled and killed a deputy running up behind him after he'd gunned down an outlaw. Most hunters never reach this level, of course, nor do they need or want to, but the few who do are something to watch in action.

It probably isn't necessary to point out that all in-home gun-handling practice should be conducted with an empty gun. Blasting the plaster off the walls is no way to endear yourself with the landlord or your nextdoor neighbor, to say nothing of your wife, who doubtless will take a dim view of such goings-on even when nothing untoward happens. Many spouses find it difficult to understand a man's feelings for guns and hunting anyway, so there's no use antagonizing yours by putting a field load of 7½s through her favorite Picasso print. Since hitting the triggers is part of the overall program, and such a practice is hard on a shotgun's firing pins, it pays to invest in a pair of snap caps—dummy shells which absorb the firing pins' energy. Use these for all gun handling practice. And it makes sense to open the action of any gun the moment you pick it up, make certain it is empty, and look through the bores to be sure there's no blockage in case you intend to load and fire it. I have no desire to sound like a preacher, but several times I've been surprised to find shells in guns that were assumed to be empty. I've had guns fire when they weren't supposed to. I've had a gun blow up when I fired it. And I've seen a guy inadvertently fire a gun into his own foot, so I know you can be surprised by these things.

Dry-firing, alone, is not a completely satisfactory way of preparing for the hunting season. Even if it gets you ready enough to give a good account of yourself, something is missing psychologically. There's no *bang* in the ears, no shove on the shoulder, nothing falling out of the sky. This is where claybird shooting enters the scene. Trap and skeet are formal, highly competitive contests for those who take them seriously, but it's not necessary to do that. Viewed as different methods of making a man a better field shot—which is what skeet at least was invented to do—they can be a great help to a hunter. It's become a cliche to tell about the programmed skeet shooter who can run a hundred straight but can't hit a pheasant or grouse to save his life. The implication here is that any fair-to-middlin' hunter can wipe the eye of one of these hotshot claybirders when the targets are live and wear real feathers. Somehow that's not the way I've seen it. I know a lot of skeet shooters, most of whom are just average in ability if judged on a competitive scale, but the vast majority of them are far better game shots than the average hunter. Why wouldn't they be? They fire hundreds, perhaps thousands, of shots to every one of the hunter's, all of them at small, fast-moving targets flying at various angles. Sure, they know almost exactly where those birds are going to fly, and exactly when and at what speed. But the fact remains that they do get the practice in gun handling and shooting, and when a bird flushes during a hunt, it pretty well has to fly along one of the paths that they're used to shooting, because skeet claybirds cover just about every direction and angle a gamebird does. That was the basic purpose of the whole thing in the beginning: to simulate the flights of wild birds so a hunter could practice on inanimate objects at a convenient time and place.

Admittedly, the simulation is not perfect. Perhaps the biggest problem is that claybirds start off fast and slow down rapidly, which is the reverse of a live bird's actions. Another problem is that you might get caught up in the competitiveness of the whole thing and find yourself wanting only to see how many consecutive birds you can break. When that happens, you find yourself calling for the bird with the gun already shouldered and cheeked, and chances are the gun will be one of the special skeet models developed to maximize your claybird-breaking abilities. There's nothing wrong with this if you enjoy it. But to use skeet as a means of improving field results it should be shot with the gun you're going to hunt with. You should call for your birds with the gun down, and the puller should deliver them in random times, rather than at the instant of the call as with competitive shooters. In other words, your rules should come close to those of International skeet, with the further handicap of using a field gun bored improved cylinder and modified, say, rather than skeet and skeet. Shot this way, which is much the way it was done a few decades back, skeet becomes a tremendous help to the hunter.

When you regularly break 20 to 23 here (which is a big nothing by competition standards) you'll find most upland bird shooting pretty easy.

Trap, too, can be a big help to the field shooter. Because the shooter stands at least 16 yards behind the trap in this game, and because the bird gets that far again before you see it, swing, and shoot, the shots are longer than in skeet. Also they come at random angles within certain limits, and this is further complicated by the shooter's moving to five different stations at five-shot intervals. The hunter who watches this a few minutes will soon see that those squirting claybirds are very closely simulating the flight patterns of wildly flushing pheasants. Obviously, this game will provide good practice for field work, particularly if shot with a hunting gun, again calling for the bird with the gun down. Sure, you won't break quite as many birds as you would with a trap gun shouldered before calling "Pull." But breaking claybirds isn't the hunter's goal in life; he wants to bust pheasants. Trap shooting will help the hunter more than he realizes. Between skeet and trap, a guy can get just about all the shots he'll ever encounter in the field.

Don't think special guns are necessary for the claybird sports. If you want to run a hundred straight, or maybe a thousand, they probably are, but for pheasant practice, they're not. A double, bored improved cylinder and modified, will serve well for both games, the modified barrel being plenty tight for 16-yard trap shooting, and open enough for the going-away shots at skeet doubles. The improved cylinder tube will handle all the close ones, if not as well as skeet #1, well enough.

It's even better practice if you load both barrels so you can fire twice at any bird if necessary, as you would at a gamebird. You can't do this in a competitive round, of course, but in practice shooting most local clubs will let you do anything you want, so long as it's safe. Once in a while you'll even corrupt one of these super-serious trapshooters into doing something like this, and he'll remember for a few minutes that there once was a time when shooting was fun. He'll probably hate you for it later, but that's life. . . .

At the local clubs, when not many shooters are around, you can also use the skeet range as a sort of quail-walk, letting a shooter wander out in the middle somewhere while the puller tries to send out a couple of birds that he can't hit. The sound of the trap tells where the first one's coming from, and the shooter will know its course in relation to himself. The sound of a second "flush" can often be hidden or disguised, either by throwing doubles or synchronizing the second bird with the gun's report, so it takes an exceptional gunner to hit them all. A hand trap can provide similar practice.

All claybird shooting prepares a hunter well for what he thinks of as "the real thing," and the cost is not really expensive when compared to that spent on any other sport: a golfer's greens fees, say, or even a ticket to sit and watch a pro football game. And we might as well recognize that there is no such thing as a something-for-nothing activity anymore; if, in fact, there ever was. Fact is, we're lucky these days if we get something for something.

Hunters living in rural areas have several other options open to them, the first being crow shooting. Time was, the number of crows was so high in many regions that anyone who wanted to make a reasonable effort could burn up more shells than he could probably afford. Such shooting was fast and fancy and was, for many gunners, an end in itself. I knew a number of them who preferred crows to gamebirds. In the last couple decades, the crow population has been on the downswing in many parts of the country (perhaps not surprisingly this decline has followed the widespread use of DDT and other chlorinated hydrocarbons which have had a proven deleterious effect upon the reproductive processes of some birds) and crows have been given some protection by the federal game agencies by way of restricted shooting seasons. Since the use of the hard pesticides also is being somewhat restricted, perhaps this bird's population will stabilize or grow; a mixed blessing, if it should occur. Though it would provide more shotgunning in the hunter's offseason, the crow is highly destructive to game and songbird eggs, and a high population of this species would most likely cause a noticeable drop in certain more desirable species. At any rate, when legal, crow shooting is a good way to keep one's shooting eye and trigger finger tuned up.

The second option is pigeons. The so-called barn pigeon is a nuisance almost everywhere. This creature is highly prolific, is found in and around practically every barn and silo in the country, and, in warm weather, can be found around such places as stone quarries.

Unlike the crow, which by comparison is an independent, remarkable, and admirable bird, the pigeon relies to a large extent on man for his sustenance, from the waste grain of the farmer to the handouts of city dwellers, many of whom seem to view him as an admirable form of wildlife. There's something pathetic about persons so far removed from nature that they can feel close to a bird that deposits its filth on the roofs, windowsills, and cornices of practically every public building in the country and then walks through it constantly, carrying various diseases and parasites with it. One country church I know of had to tear down its bellsteeple because no way could be found to keep pigeons out, and their droppings were overpowering. In a building where I once worked, they had not only fouled all the windowsills but also left behind lice which worked their way through the tiny joints around the closed windows and into the offices. At the same time that this was occurring, many of the office workers spent their noon hours in the adjoining park, feeding these birds parts of their lunches. Big-hearted bird-lovers; it would have made a lot more sense to feed the birds strychnine.

Trying to rid cities of this bird costs taxpayers many millios of dollars each year, and it's a losing battle. If there's a lasting solution to the city pigeon problem, I've never heard of it. The only good thing I can think of about this bird is that it makes a great target for the shotgunner. And though it's obviously impossible to shoot these critters within city limits, it quite often can be arranged to shoot them on nearby farms or on flyways between the city and farm where they move in and out to feed. Sometimes this can provide gunning much as crows used to. Early last dove season Ted Them and I were sweltering in the early September sun, getting only an occasional shot at the mourners, when pigeons started coming in. I was leaning against a power line pole in the middle of a weed field about a mile and a half out of town, and for some reason a flock of pigeons kept insisting on coming in there. I had two boxes of shells with me, less a few I'd expended on doves, and two more boxes in the car, and in a short time I'd run through them all. I had pigeons lying all around that pole, some of them heavy as grouse, and I'd probably be shooting yet if the shells had held out. Sometimes these critters are hard to discourage, but most of the time they don't offer this kind of gunning, unless the dead birds act as decoys and they haven't been shot up too badly in the recent past. I didn't think the dead ones could be seen well from the air in the weeds, but maybe they could.

I remember watching a friend turn in an even more impressive account on pigeons one summer afternoon. We had been invited to help thin the population on a large farm, and somehow or another my buddy found himself sitting right out in the open in a strip of clover on a gentle hillside. He had no cover or camouflage, though his clothing was neutral colored and his seated position didn't skyline him or really attract too much attention. Nevertheless, it was a bit weird to watch those pigeons. He'd dropped a couple early, before they realized they were being shot at, and tossed them about 20 yards in front of him on a bare contour strip. Before long, others started coming in, in singles mostly. From my position a couple of hundred yards away, I could see them going over high above, then they'd spot his dead ones and float down in a big tightening spiral, and just as they flared in to land, hanging maybe a yard off the ground, his gun would pop, feathers would puff, and another pigeon was added to the decoys. I don't know how many he took this way—he shot till he ran out of shells, and I never saw him miss—but it was between fifty and seventy-five, and all of them were lying within an area you could almost cover with a blanket. This particular episode was no great help toward improved pheasant shooting, but it was interesting and shows the kind of action you can enjoy at times on pigeons.

On the skeet or trap range, the problem of what to do with the gun between shots is slight. You just wait with it empty until you're ready to call for the bird. Even shooting pests such as crows and pigeons, it's likely you'll be doing little moving around with a loaded gun. But in pheasant hunting, you can darn well carry that thing up hill and down, through all kinds of cover, often with other hunters nearby, for hours at a stretch between shots. When a chance comes it may be completely unexpected. Yet, if you are to have a successful trip, in a very short period of time you have to recognize the target, decide if the shot is safe to attempt, swing that gun into firing position from whatever carrying position you are using at the moment, and slap off a shot.

Actually, there's nothing difficult about this procedure, at least about the shooting part, and yet a significant percentage of hunters never do seem to master it. Often this is due to the way they carry their guns. When shots are few and far between, some gunners lose interest. They poke along half-heartedly with the gun drooping or carried in one hand at arm's length, occasionally it is even slanted back across the shoulder, trigger guard down, as a soldier marches with his rifle in a parade. If there is a worse way to carry a shotgun than that, it will take more time than I can spare to figure out what it is. In the first place, it isn't safe. Every time the hunter changes direction a bit the muzzle swings in an arc to cover most everybody in the area, assuming anyone is crazy enough to stay in the same field with such a kook. In the second place, it's impossible to get a gun into action from that carry in anything like reasonable time.

It's understandable why hunters adopt such carries. If they are not used to carrying a gun for a long period of time, their arms get tired and they experiment with various ways of easing the strain. Early in the season, elbows ache from being crooked for hours, taking the strain of the gun's weight. Letting the gun hang in one hand, arm straight, is a normal thing to do, so far as one's muscles are concerned, for it gets the kinks out. Normally, this can be safe enough, as the muzzle is pointing straight forward. However, it's a bit slow to get into action as the gun has so far to travel to the shoulder, and the hand is at the gun's balance from where it must move front or back, depending on whether it's going to wind up on the fore-end or the grip. This works best if the gun is carried in the left hand (for a

For reasons of safety, gunners hunting together must be constantly aware of the other's location. If one is a southpaw, the problem is simplified because it's natural to carry the guns angling away from each other.

right-handed shooter), as it is simply swept upward across the front of the body, the right hand grabbing the grip and pulling the butt into the shoulder as the left hand moves forward to point the gun.

Despite the necessity of getting into action quickly, the first requisite for a carry is not convenience for the shot but safety. It's fairly difficult to shoot yourself with a shotgun (unless you do something extremely stupid like dragging a loaded gun through a fence with the muzzle pointing at your belly), but it's awfully easy to shoot someone else. All it takes is a moment's forgetfulness and a bit of bad luck. The wrong carry simply makes it easy for all these conditions to come together. Through the years, millions of words have been written on safe gun handling, but they can all be boiled down into one sentence: Never let a gun muzzle point at anything you don't want to shoot. If that muzzle is always pointed in a safe direction, even if the gun fires unexpectedly, nobody is going to get hurt. Too often, hunters carry guns so their muzzles wave back and forth across their buddies with every step. This happens when a gun is draped across the front of the body over a crooked arm, the muzzle at almost a right angle to the direction of walking. This is quite likely the most dangerous way there is to carry a gun. The barrel is almost parallel to the ground, which means it won't send its shot charge over a nearby hunter's head as the also-dangerous "right-shoulder arms" carry will occasionally do; and the muzzle's angular movement caused by walking puts almost everything on the gunner's left side in danger. It might be permissible for the man on the left end of a line to use this carry, or if right- and lefthanded gunners are hunting together, they can line up so their muzzles are pointing away from each other. There are better carries from all aspects except possibly comfort, however, so it's just as well not to get into the habit of using this one.

A basic rule in gun carrying is to keep the muzzle pointed forward, or essentially so. That's the way the hunter is looking most of the time, so he'll see another person who suddenly appears in that direction and can adjust his gun accordingly, and so on. A muzzle pointed off to one side can easily be covering another hunter he isn't even aware of. It's safer if the gun barrel is pointed upward or downward, as well as to the front, for an accidental discharge then will probably cause no harm. Upward is usually preferable as it keeps the muzzle out of the mud or snow in case of a stumble.

It's difficult to keep the muzzle forward with a two-hand carry. If one is not careful, the gun will naturally rest at the army's port-arms position, the barrel slanting upward across the chest, actually pointing directly left except for the angle. The only way it can point forward is by pulling the butt back alongside the hip with the right hand, the left extending out stiffly as in bayonet drill; not exactly a practical way of moving through the brush with a gun. The fact is, most of the time a two-hand carry is neither necessary nor desirable. Sometimes it's useful for shoving through thick cover, if you don't mind the gun getting scratched up, but even here it's best to hold it vertically in front of the center of the body, one hand on the grip and the other on the fore-end. It separates the cover that way and is still fast to get into operation. The natural time to use a two-hand carry is when moving in on pointed birds or when waiting for an imminent flush. In either case the muzzle should be pointing to the front, the butt tucked between the upper arm and the rib cage, and both hands at or near the normal shooting position.

There are several good one-hand carries that are useful for most upland hunting situations. In the first, the firing hand grips the wrist of the stock with the barrel slanting up across the shoulder, guard up and finger across it to protect the trigger. Because the angle between the stock and barrel is reversed from that of the right-shoulder-arms carry, the muzzle points nearly vertically now instead of almost flat. It cannot point at another shooter. Even when the gunner turns completely around, the muzzle does no more than describe a small circle toward the sky. The safety factor is thus satisfied, and at the same time the gun is very fast to get into operation from this carry. Jerking downward with the carrying hand (at the same time hunching the shoulder in the opposite direction if the gun is a heavy one) snaps the muzzle up, over and down in a smooth arc, the butt rising to its seat in the shoulder, the fore-end slapping into the rising left hand at about the time the gun is pointing at the target. The safety is thumbed off during the process, and the gun fires almost without conscious thought.

In a similar one-hand carry the right hand serves the same function as above, but the barrel points straight up, the butt resting on the bottom row of shells on the front of the vest. This is just as safe as the other carry and even faster to fire from. The right hand tilts the gun into shooting position at the same time as it raises the butt to the shoulder and the left hand moves out to take the fore-end. Someone used to sell a leather cup that fastened on the belt or to a shoulder strap and provided a resting place for the gun butt. Such a device would be convenient for anyone not suited by the shell arrangement described. Sometimes it's convenient just to carry the gun vertically in one hand, either by the grip with the firing hand or the fore-end with the other hand. These again keep the muzzle pointing safely and at the same time let one arm rest.

In times past, probably because there were more rabbit hunters then than now, it was common to see a hunter mooching along, eyes studying every bit of cover as he looked for a sitting bunny's eye, gun draped over his elbow, butt beneath his shoulder, and muzzle pointing toward the ground a bit ahead of his feet. This is a comfortable carry, but slow to get into action from, particularly on a rising target. A few old gunners have mastered the trick of flipping the gun upward with their forearm and then, while it literally hung in the air for a moment, grabbing it with their hands in the proper firing positions, shouldering, and firing. That takes practice! All in all, I've always regarded this method of carrying as one best reserved for a man hunting alone in an open field where game offers more time for the shot.

Depending on the situations of cover, terrain, muscle fatigue, likelihood of seeing game at a particular moment, and the direction from which it will probably appear, etc., all these and other gun carries are used. In the end, personal experience governs the choice.

The purpose of carrying a gun, of course, is to shoot something with it, so some comments on hitting may be useful. The benefits of claybird shooting have been discussed, but useful as skeet and trap are, they do not fully match actual hunting situations. In the field you never know just when or where a bird will appear, the direction it will take, or what its exact speed will be. By comparison, in skeet shooting you know all these things very precisely, and in trap shooting, although you do not know the exact direction a claybird is going to fly, you always know the point it's going to fly from. Therefore, you know exactly where to watch for it and, knowing the extreme limits within which it must fly, you position yourself to cover the full field without the necessity of making an extreme change in attitude.

Positioning yourself to fully control the space through which the target must move is of utmost importance to good shotgunning. It's impossible to reach a high standard of shooting proficiency without practicing this. What this amounts to in the field is shifting the feet in whatever way is necessary at the instant a bird is sighted so that the body is almost square with the bird, or more accurately, almost square with that point where the bird will be when the shot is fired. This done, the body is easily balanced and free to swing the gun. This puts the gunner in the same relationship to his live target that the trap or skeet shooter is to his claybird. Thus situated, hitting is comparatively easy. Admittedly, there are times when kills can be made without attaining the ideal attitude. Sometimes the hunter is so entangled in laurel, cat briars, honeysuckle, or whatever, or his footing is so precarious, that when a bird goes out he just cannot make any adjustment in foot placement. He simply swings as well as he can and shoots. If the bird's flight path happens to be within a space that he can cover by twisting his shoulders or body, he can well make a clean kill. If the flight is outside the total accommodation of all his joints, however, that bird is impossible for him to hit, even though it would have been a perfectly easy chance if he were able to shift his feet. When such a situation arises the importance of the feet to good shooting becomes obvious. They are normally moved subconsciously to cover the target; only when it's impossible to shift them does the value of their placement become glaringly evident.

It would be possible to describe in detail exactly where each foot should be for any kind of shot, how each should move during the swing, and how the body weight upon them shifts. Churchill does this in his *Game Shooting,* which is quite likely the most instructive book on shotgunning available. However, I doubt if reiterating his instructions in detail is greatly helpful. Quite often the reader feels confused rather than enlightened by the seemingly intricate movements. And the truth is, it just isn't necessary to think about all that stuff for the simple reason that it's all automatic. After all, we've been walking on our two feet for our entire lives; they respond to the demands put on them by the weight of our bodies, shifting and accommodating as necessary to support whatever is happening above. What I'm trying to say is this: Once you have moved your feet so that your body is in the proper attitude toward the target, you don't have to worry about what movements they're going to go through as you swing and shoot. They'll do whatever is necessary. If you start trying to control mentally each minute change, you'll get so stiffened and fouled up you'll be falling flat on your face. The trick is to get into a position where you can easily move the gun to cover any flight path of the target; then relax and swing.

Keeping the gun moving is one of the most important elements of wing shooting, perhaps the most important, for nothing happens instantaneously. It takes time for a trigger finger to twitch in response to some signal from the human nervous system, time for the lockwork of the gun to function, time for the primer to ignite the gunpowder and for that solid powder to convert into gas and build the pressure that squirts a shot charge down a barrel, and time for that shot to cross the space intervening between the gun muzzle and the bird. Even though the total elapsed time of all these intervals is small, it's enough that a moving bird will be well beyond the pattern's outermost fringes if the gun is simply aimed at it and fired.

Very few shots can be made with a motionless gun; it may even be safe to say that none can be made consistently. The only exception that comes to mind is a target which appears motionless in relation to the gunner, such as a bird coming directly at the gun or going straight away from it. On such chances, it's possible to put the front sight right on the target and shoot, aiming much as with a rifle. However, true straightaway shots are rare in the field. Quite a few chances look like straightaways, but actually a slight angle is common to most of these, and it often is great enough that the gunner who holds dead on with a motionless gun shoots behind or gets a tail-end hit and a crippled bird. It is easy to take shots like these with a moving gun, and in the long run that's the best way because it eliminates the problem of not consciously recognizing the angle, and it maintains a consistent shooting style, always an aid to hitting.

Swing is to shotgunning what follow-through is to golfing or baseball. It is obviously impossible to stop the golf club a microsecond after it has imparted its energy and have the ball do what you want it to, despite the fact that the applied energy is the only thing

Hitting pheasants, or most any upland game, isn't normally difficult. Just swing through the target and slap the trigger as the gun muzzle passes it.

working on the ball. To stop the club in that instant requires anticipating the moment of impact exactly and stopping the swing of the club as soon as it has hit the ball. This cannot be done. Just as you must swing the golf club through the ball, you must swing the gun muzzle through the target. Firing the gun is analogous to hitting the ball; each occurs during the swing and without it the swing is pointless; nevertheless, neither actually interrupts the swing to any measurable degree. If the swing is interrupted, the golf ball doesn't go into the cup or the shot charge doesn't hit the bird. And so, while shooting the bird is the ultimate purpose of shotgunning, swinging the gun is what makes consistent hitting possible.

For the experienced hunter, the swing begins the instant the gun moves out of its carrying position toward the shoulder. Unlike the formal claybird shooter, the hunter doesn't raise his gun, cheek it consciously, gaze out along the rib, call for the bird, and then swing. Rather, he still has the gun down when the bird appears, or at least when he hears it flush. At the first sight or sound, he shifts his feet to face the bird, leaning a bit forward so that he can swing the gun more easily and control its recoil better. Simultaneously, the gun butt is moving toward his shoulder. However—and this is the important part—even before it is fully seated there, even before the fore-end is

Sam flushes rooster toward Bashline, who turns and takes it going away. Sometimes this maneuver makes an easier shot . . . and it usually is less destructive.

grasped by his left hand, his body already is swinging with the bird; the gun is tracking through the plane of the bird's flight path, and his head is tilting slightly to cheek the stock properly. There is no pause anywhere in this operation. Even as the butt settles into the hollow of his shoulder and the left hand tightens on the fore-end to control any bounce and help take up recoil, the firing finger slaps the trigger. The gun continues its swing, making an immediate second shot easy if necessary. Sometimes the second shot will be fired even if unneeded, simply because the whole procedure has been made so automatic by those hours of gun drill in the home that it's impossible to break the sequence. That's okay. A lot of pheasants can take some extra killing, and it's worth the cost of an occasional shot up bird to maintain your shooting rhythm.

In this method of shooting, you swing from behind the bird, overtake it, and hit the trigger as the gun muzzle passes the bird's head. At normal ranges, the white ring around a pheasant's neck is a conspicuous mark that serves as a signal for shooting. You don't have to worry about the amount of lead, for the speed of the swing is largely governed by the target's speed, and when you try to shoot the bird's head off, your reaction time plus the mechanical time factors involved automatically give you the proper allowance. On incoming birds, you swing up from below, firing just as the muzzle blots out the target. On those rare chances where the bird is moving directly in, the gun moves in a vertical plane; where a slight angle is involved, the gun's path accommodates for this, the horizontal factor increasing with the angle to reach its greatest value on birds crossing at right angles.

For several reasons, a lot of hunters have trouble with incoming birds. There is a tendency to let them get too close, probably due to the subconscious feeling that it's easier to hit something near at hand than some distance away. Yet a bird coming to the gun is much easier to hit 35 yards out, say, than it is when directly overhead. The gun delivers its most useful pattern size at about that distance. (It covers a comparatively large size but still has good shot density there.) Despite the bird's absolute speed, its movement in relation to the gunner is much slower at 35 yards away than when it approaches the vertical; thus the gun's upward movement can be slower, and the shooter has more time to do what he wants. The closer the bird is, the faster the gun has to swing. When the bird passes directly overhead it's almost impossible to catch up with it; not only because of its speed but also because there's a limit to how far the hips can shove ahead, the shoulders back, and the left hand reach up and back to shove the barrels, to say nothing of how the stock moves out of contact with the cheek. After an incoming bird has reached a certain point, it's a lot easier to turn around and take it as an outgoer than to try to hit it coming in. Some hunters also have trouble with incomers because, in order to hit them, they have to fire when the barrels have blotted out the target, and shooting at an invisible bird upsets them psychologically. They know that's how it must be done, but when they swing up they can get that muzzle only as far as the bird. It stops there, the gun goes off, and they shoot behind.

I always had more trouble with outgoing birds, those that came over my head from behind. For years it seemed unnatural to shoot under the target, but from a spot behind and below an outgoer that's the only way it can be hit. Again, claybirds are helpful. The highhouse bird from the number one skeet station duplicates this type of shot and makes practice easy. An early instructor, advising me how to hit the skeet target, said, "Just pretend it's a pheasant and take the feet off," and unknowingly solved my hunting problem, which was of more interest to me than breaking the claybirds. This instructive comment has made it easy for me to take such shots, for it always comes to mind as needed, reminding me that these chances are not difficult.

Steeply rising ringnecks, taken from behind, are easy too, if the swing goes all the way through them so the load centers on the forward part of the bird. A straightaway shot on a big old rooster sometimes provides killing problems, as the vitals are protected by the trailing legs and the intestines. However, a flushing ringneck often goes up at a steep angle so that you're shooting into the top of the back. The vital organs have little protection here, just feathers and a thin rib cage, so the bird is easily killed.

A typical example of this shot occurred many seasons ago when I was hunting with Ray Harley along Catawissa Creek in east-central Pennsylvania. Ray raised registered beagles, and we were in good cottontail country, yet the way the dog was working made me think he was on a bird. I was standing on a little bluff above the creek and the dog was moving toward me through a skinny bit of cover along the water. The cover ran out at the bluff, so anything in it would have to climb a bare bank, swim, or fly. It was a rooster that came out, thrashing upward above the creek, and I centered it in the back for the instant kill typical of such shots. Naturally the bird came down in the middle of the creek, which was hip deep at that point and chilly, for it was late November. I'm certain about the depth and temperature, because it was either wade out and get that critter or walk away and leave it.

A bird that flushes with its breast toward you is a less desirable shot. The vitals are protected by the thick breast muscles, and though this won't save them at the range where such chances normally are taken, the pellets drive feathers into the meat, quite often shoot it up badly, and in general cause more destruction of the portions you want to eat.

Most upland game is best taken with a fast swing-through. Many writers have described this as "hosing" the target or "wiping it out" as with a garden hose or a paintbrush, and that's about how it's done. Just mount the gun, swinging as you do, with eyes focused on the target, and hit the trigger when the muzzle passes through the bird.

There are other methods. Spot shooting or what some gunners call snap shooting; and pointing them out, a sustained lead approach, are the two styles most discussed. In spot shooting the gunner simply snaps off a shot from a motionless gun, directing it at some place in space where he expects ("hopes" is a better word) the bird to be when the pattern arrives. If the range is short and the bird's flight at a narrow angle to the hunter, so that he essentially is almost grazing the edge of the target with his shot, this method can work very well. On more severe angles at longer range, where a spot some feet ahead of the bird must be selected and hit, kill percentages drop off rapidly. The reasons are simple. Nobody knows exactly how far a given bird will move in the time it takes to deliver the shot to the place where their paths will intercept, nor even how long it will take the shot to get there. You're working with all unknown factors; the only thing you're sure of is your desire to hit the bird. Such shots are made occasionally. That pattern has a big diameter and is stretched out lengthwise for some feet, and a successful shot like this can keep you walking on clouds for a week. But most such kills are more good luck than good management, and spot shooting is best reserved for those chances in impossible cover when there's no other way to bust a cap. When you hear the bird thump down—if you can see it fall you probably didn't have to spot shoot it—figure that the Red Gods were in a good mood that day.

Pointing out birds is a better method than spot shooting at anything beyond pointblank range ... but not much. In this system the shooter gets his gun muzzle somewhere ahead of the bird, the amount corresponding to whatever he thinks the proper lead is, keeps it swinging at a rate to maintain that lead, and shoots. This is the method which always seems logical to persons who have never fired a shot at a moving target but who have been exposed to grade school mathematics. These would-be rooster shooters delight in formulating charts, graphs, and tables showing average speeds of all species of gamebirds, average reaction times of hunters, lockwork, powder ignition times, average shot velocities over all hunting ranges at 10-yard intervals, and distances each bird will travel during a specific time period based on the above, etc. Given such data they blithely proceed to work out the required leads for each and every chance possible in the uplands, the lowlands, the marshes, and wherever else feathered critters fly. The theory behind their approach is that all the unknown time intervals prior to firing (reaction time and mechanics) are eliminated, and choosing the proper lead eliminates the problem of shot flight time. The only thing is, this method seldom if ever works. The big kicker is choosing the proper

How to Hit Him

lead. This is extremely difficult. No one can tell for certain just by looking at a bird how far away it is, how fast it's moving, or it's speed relative to the shooter, which is not the same as its actual flight speed if it's at an angle other than directly crossing. Since these things vary with every shot, and the whole thing is further complicated by the impossibility of knowing just how far ahead of a bird you're actually holding, dropping birds by the pointing out method becomes a more miss than hit thing for the majority of hunters. The human mind is not a computer, and even a computer cannot give correct answers if it has not been fed accurate data on which to work.

It's far simpler to hit a moving target with a shotgun if you simply swing through it from behind, tracking its path with the gun, and hit the trigger as the muzzle passes the bird's beak. I know I've said that before, but it's worth repeating. So far as I'm concerned, it's the only logical way to shoot a shotgun. It eliminates all that malarkey about distances and time and lets you concentrate on the bird and kill it. You just swing and shoot. It's a system that works, and it's easy to learn. A good example is my daughter Peej (short for Patricia Jo). She'd been doing some benchrest shooting with a rifle off and on from about age 10, and just after turning 13 she wanted to start shooting a shotgun. The two games obviously required different techniques. I was glad she was interested and happened to have a new gun I thought would be just her size, a 26-inch Ithaca SKB 20-gauge bored skeet and skeet. All that was required to get an acceptable fit was removal of the factory-installed recoil pad.

We started with a ground-mounted trap. After a half dozen straightaways so she would have some confidence she could hit targets in the air, I moved the trap so it was throwing the birds at a modest angle. "Just swing through it and shoot," I told her, and that was all that was necessary. She hit most of them, even when I mixed up the angles on her. We then moved to the regulation skeet range. A little indoctrination and the same instruction—swing and shoot—and she was busting those with fair regularity. I never once tried to explain the mysteries of lead to her, and I wouldn't let anyone else do it. Skeet shooters are hell on telling anyone who will listen precisely how many feet of lead each bird takes from every position. This might be all right if all you want to do is break skeet birds. If you wanted to, I'm sure you could even work out a system of aiming at some specific point in the bird's path, timing the shot from a motionless gun so it would intersect the grooved claybird. But I wanted her to be able to hit random-flying pheasants as well as claybirds, and the way to do that is by moving the gun. So I emphasized that to the point that some of her misses were ahead of the bird. She shot behind on some because she realized she was too far ahead and stopped the gun. We discussed that, and after awhile we got to station eight, which is not tough for a veteran skeet shooter, but which looks impossible to most beginners. The bird comes pretty fast and due to your firing position in the middle of the field, time seems nonexistent. I was standing behind her, watching her gun handling, and feeding her shells. I had ten shells in my pouch when we got to this station. "You gotta swing fast on this one," I told her. She missed the first one. "Watch the bird's path and swing through it," I said. She shot ahead of the second. (Lord, what reactions teenagers have!) "Just swing and shoot," I told her. She broke the next one. And then she powdered seven more. Now, this might not be great stuff by an old skeet shooter's standards, but eight consecutive hits at station 8 for a first-time shooter, age 13, is not bad in my book. And she did it because she didn't try to calculate any lead or do anything else mental. She just swung the gun and shot.

That's what all shotgunning comes down to.

9

Some Thoughts on Equipment

Pheasant hunters are not noted for sartorial splendor; at least not those of my acquaintance—particularly myself. This used to bother my wife, Terry, considerably. "The least you can do is get a new pair of pants once in awhile," she'd say. And then when I did so she would ask, "Why do you have to cut the bottoms off?" Women have a hard time understanding hunting husbands (that is, husbands who hunt), particularly if they do not come from a hunting family. But after a decade or so of seasons passed, Terry's comments tapered off, and now she rarely says anything more disparaging than "It'd be nice if you got a jacket or something from Abercrombie & Fitch this year." I've tried to explain that such highbrow houses are patronized only by grouse and woodcock hunters, but I'm afraid I've failed at this. Somehow Terry thinks hunting clothes are to be looked at. I think of them only as necessities for keeping me warm, reasonably dry, and protected from the greenbriars and multiflora rose thickets.

Well, that's probably not completely true. I haven't taken time to think it through, but I realize there's some urge or instinct that makes me prefer somewhat disreputable clothes to hunt in. I'm not alone in this. It's safe to say that a majority of our upland game hunters take the field wearing clothes they wouldn't wash the car in, and various superior-type outdoor writers have been annoyed by this through he years. One who comes to mind, perhaps because I read him when I was young and impressionable, is Capt. Paul Curtis, who, in his *Guns and Gunning,* took Americans to task for this characteristic as far back as the early 1930s. The good captain of course was highly influenced by things British. (He even dedicated his book to His Grace, the Duke of Montrose.) Because of his and similar writings it's long been religiously believed in this country that the upper class of that tight little isle *always* do their driven grouse gunning in tweed knickerbocker suits with matching caps and mackintoshes. However, if you read Churchill's chapter, "Clothes and Accessories," in *Game Shooting* the suggestion comes to mind that shooters' preferences for comfortable, even oddball, clothing are much the same no matter where gunning is done or what the theoretical traditions are. Somehow I feel that the observations of old gunmaker-shooter-coach Churchill more accurately portray the way things are than do some others who tend to write about the way they think things ought to be . . . a clear example of the sociologist's ideal-real dichotomy.

One reason hunters cling to their brush-whipped clothing, other than comfort, is a sort of reverse snobbery, of course. It sets them apart from the neophytes in the way that Willie and Joe, Bill Mauldin's rumpled, unwashed, unshaved GI's of World War II fame, were set apart from their eager, fatigues-pressed replacements and from the pretty-faced flyboys. They have a "been there" look that can't be bought, must be earned. Childish? Sure, a little bit. But that's human nature, and we might as well face it.

There are other reasons. When you think about it a bit, the almost inevitable conclusion is that some of us, subconsciously perhaps, are fighting a rearguard battle against the female influence that's pervading all spheres of life. Hunting was undoubtedly the first great male activity, and I believe it will be the last, but even here the women are putting on the pressure. They don't want to take part—at least very few of them do—but they want to control as much of it as they can. Some of them want to eliminate hunting entirely, while others simply are making their weight felt. I doubt if they do this

Leather and heavy canvas make the best gear for pheasant hunting. Here, Don Lewis, gunwriter for *Pennsylvania Game News*, and Bob Bell both wear leather-faced pants, but Lewis chooses a conventional sleeved jacket with integral game bag, while Bell prefers a game vest worn over a heavy pigskin shirt. Buckskin gloves protect hands from brambles and make no-slip contact with gun.

intentionally; rather, it's the nature of the female beast, a normal extension of the feminine urge which has brought humanity to what today is pathetically, or comically, called civilization.

There are individuals, even among the hunting group, who advocate neatness to the point of dandyness, claiming that a ragged-tail appearance provides fuel for the anti-hunters who point us out as the horrible examples among mankind. As it happens, I have personally been taken to task by various so-called friends of animals, and I've got to say there is no one in this world that I'd rather offend. If the day comes that I let a bunch like that dictate what I'm to wear or to do or to say, I'll cash in my chips completely.

And so a few of us, primarily the roughneck group which thinks the ringneck is a gamebird, fight back in one of the few ways left open to us, deliberately clinging to our briar-frayed britches long after they've earned retirement so that, in a minor way at least, we can maintain our independence. The time may come when the pheasant attains a ranking in the minds of hunters similar to that of, say, the woodcock, and those who chase after him may feel obligated to affect a respectable appearance. But something will have gone out of pheasant hunting.

So what is needed in the way of equipment for this game? Well, if you have a gun, shells, and a license, you can hunt pheasants. Choice of clothing is not your biggest problem. I've seen a lot of men, particularly farmers stealing a few hours away from their chores, in overalls, gumboots, and an old jacket. In his later years, in good weather, my dad used to sneak along in carpet slippers! He never suggested it, but I always had a hunch he was expecting me to boot the birds out of the thick stuff—which was okay with me, because that's where I always liked to be. Still, some equipment is more suitable than other kinds, and through the years I've reached some conclusions about it which may help beginning hunters. Not much use talking to the old-timers; they've got their own ideas: for instance, a farmer's choice of overalls and Dad's fondness for comfortable slippers.

Despite the fact that it's become a cliche to say boots are an outdoorsman's most important piece of equipment, it's true. Given the proper boots you can manage most hunting situations with any sort of old clothes, because you can get around. With ill-fitting boots you soon will be so blistered that you just can't maneuver, so we might as well start at the bottom and work up.

Boots for pheasant hunting come in three general types: rubber, leather, and a combination of the two, leather-topped rubbers or shoe pacs. A few generations back, boots that reached to just below the knee were common. Hunters then often wore breeches which tucked into the boot tops or ended just below the knee, so the high boots were necessary for leg protection and, if waterproof, made it possible to wade streams of ordinary depth. There's something to be said for that; nevertheless, in recent decades the trend has been toward lower, lighter boots worn in combination with conventional design pants. Saving of weight is the routine explanation here, but it's debatable if there's an actual saving when the change in pant type is considered. Personally I favor eight- or nine-inch boots, for I never liked the feel of a tightly laced high top or the way breeches cramped my calf muscle.

One or two hunting friends like ankle-height boots because of their even lighter weight, but I'm skeptical about these. You need the protection of leather when kicking the brush, and it's my impression that ankle-height boots feel heavier than the eight-inchers simply because the weight is taken on the top of the foot. It seems to have more effect here than the few ounces more of the upland type which are primarily lifted by the lower leg.

Shoes of street height are useless in any kind of ground cover, even with droopy pant bottoms, because normal walking movements raise these enough to expose the ankles. Even ankle-high styles don't protect the lower leg enough. The eight- or nine-inch top typical of many makers' boots today is the best compromise between weight and protection for ordinary upland hunting. Local conditions might suggest a greater height, but there's little point in going much lower.

Most hunters choose between leather and rubber on the basis of the weather, leather when it's dry, rubber when it's wet. That seems logical, but it doesn't work for me. Years ago I found out that my feet perspire so much in rubber that, insofar as wet feet go, I might as well be wearing leather when it rains. So I do. As far as I'm concerned, rubber boots are an abomination. They not only retain perspiration but in anything like normal temperatures their imperviousness creates a heating effect that induces athlete's foot. Furthermore, they give no support at all to the ankles and little to the foot. They always feel clumsy to me, and perhaps because I've never found a pair that fits as snugly as a laced leather boot. They often feel as if they're not quite with me; sort of moving a quarter-step after my feet do. That bothers me. Maybe rubber boots have none of these effects on you. If so, you're lucky, and you can wade shallow creeks dry shod. Or you can go a step further, wear hipboots, wade deep creeks, and get to productive little spots where most hunters never tread. Except guys like me; remember that rooster in Catawissa Creek?

Shoe pacs are a bit better. Their rubber bottoms are proof against wet grass, mud, etc., and their leather tops can be laced snugly around the ankles for some support. Most makes are built deep enough (from sole to instep) to permit a felt insole, which not all rubber boots will do. This absorbs perspiration rather well and can be dried at night for use the next day. Pacs come in all heights, but again the medium-low version is usually most suitable. A corrugated crepe rubber sole for years was standard on pacs, and it's still a good choice, but newer ones are being offered with Vibram-types. These have heavy lugs that provide excellent traction on most surfaces but they're heavy and they tend to pick up mud during small game hunting. Though not waterproof in the sense that all-rubber boots are, pacs will turn water enough, if properly greased, to wade low streams if you don't poke along.

The all-leather, moccasin-toe, low boot as made by Bass, Russell, Red Wing, and others, has become the standard upland hunting shoe. My first pair of this type was by Bass, and after wearing out quite a few pairs of various makes I've never found any I liked more, though I feel some others are as good. That first pair, when I was about 15, formed some kind of pinnacle in my young hunting life. There was something superior about them, something I could feel deep inside, even if I couldn't explain it. They weren't perfect, I found that out soon. The soles were the problem. They were smooth leather, and this soon buffed to a slickness that could make staying upright on a sidehill a problem. But as time went on various other materials replaced the smooth leather until now there isn't much about such boots that I want to change. The Vibram soles are available here, too, but much as I like these for big game hunting, particularly in the rough Rocky Mountain country, say, I don't find them necessary in pheasant cover. The original type, intended to protect the feet in rocky country as well as provide traction, is heavier than necessary. A lighter weight version, with a shallower tread and more flexible sole, is preferable. Actually, any composition sole with a corrugated surface will serve for the type of country where pheasants are found.

Some authorities have condemned the wedge-type composition sole which has no separate heel, claiming it will permit you to skid ski-like on some slopes, and this comment seems logical when you simply look at these. But I used such soles on a pair of Red Wings, and in the four years it took me to wear them out, I never had this happen. I don't believe boots with this style of bottom can be resoled, but this isn't often a factor of importance as the tops normally go bad before the bottoms. The folded seam of the moccasin toe tends to wear out, the leather itself as well as the stitching, from kicking through brush. Since the advent of nylon thread, the stitching usually lasts longer than the leather. In the good old days I spent more than an occasional hour re-sewing this part of such boots.

One lightweight pair I tried, which advertises somewhat exotic soft leather uppers, went bad even quicker; not on the seam but at the front curve of the boot where it rounds off along the outer edge of the foot. A hard season's hunting wore the leather completely through here in a spot like a big bunion. These were very comfortable boots to walk in, or stand around in, but for brush-busting they didn't amount to much. I've never had a pair of Bass, Russell, or Red Wings go bad that way.

Some hunters dislike the lack of support moccasin-type boots give the arches. I've never had that trouble, but I can see where it might be a problem. Boots with higher heels and soles, more similar to those one is used to in street shoes, are available. Dunham makes some that are liked by friends, and more extreme versions such as logger's boots can be obtained in the Pacific Northwest. I'd go slow on these for upland hunting, though. They're specialized equipment, designed for specific conditions and terrain a long way removed from the cornfields of the Midwest. Some Idaho friends wear them for elk hunting (when they aren't wearing basketball sneakers over a couple pairs of wool socks for pussyfooting through the mountain mahogany thickets!) and I wore them for several years when setting chokers out there, but they do take some getting used to. Few Easterners are going to like them, despite their quality material and workmanship and practicality on their own turf.

Regular greasing with one of the commercial preparations helps maintain life in boot leather as well as repel mosture, and it's a good habit to treat them regularly. An old toothbrush is fine for filling rows of stitching and, upper-sole crevices. Before greasing, the leather should be wiped clean. Don't forget to loosen the laces so seeds, weeds, and other assorted items gathered along the tongue during the day can be swept out. If necessary, the leather should be dried; not by close contact with a flame or intense heat though. There's no quicker way than that to ruin a good pair of boots. If merely damp, they'll dry overnight at room temperature; if soaked through, they can be wiped thoroughly with an old towel and then be hung up wherever warm air circulates. Sometimes it takes several days to properly dry them. No matter what, don't try to rush it or the leather will be burned and the boots ruined. If much hunting in wet weather is done, it pays to use several pairs alternately.

Various silicone dressings are now available and they work well, particularly on new boots which have no cracks in the leather, and they are easy to apply as they come in spray cans.

I like boots of a size that will comfortably permit wearing two pairs of medium-weight wool socks when they are snugly laced. This much insulation will keep the feet warm in almost any weather a pheasant shooter faces, protects against stone bruises, and at the same time helps keep the feet dry when the weather is warmer, as perspiration tends to move outward. Wool shrinks if subjected to high temperatures, as in hot wash water or fast drying, so it's a good idea to avoid these. Tight socks can curl your toes both literally and figuratively, and neither way is any fun. In fact, it's pure misery. Despite its many virtues, wool does not wear well at the heels of socks, so buy those reinforced with nylon here. They're worth their extra cost. They need be boot height only, but knee-high styles protect the shins when the pant leg lifts up during various activities. I've never found a suitable way of keeping high socks from dribbling down, unless long underwear is being worn, in which case safety pins do the job. Garters cut off circulation.

Nylon or other manmade laces outwear those of rawhide, but I don't like them as much. They don't want to stay tied and in general have a synthetic feel and appearance which bothers me. But they are strong and durable. Best way I've found to lace boots is to pull them up snugly as far as the ankle and tie off with a square knot. This keeps everything firm and non-slipping on the foot, which gives good control and prevents rubbing. Boots that fit properly, are broken in, and are tied as they should be will never give a blister or raw spot. If they do, something is wrong and should be corrected. From the ankle up, the lacing does not have to be overly tight. It definitely should not bind the leg muscles. Running the laces through every hole helps keep trash out of the tongue crevices, and lacing all the way to the top keeps seeds, etc., from getting down inside the boot. A square knot will usually hold here in rawhide laces, and if the lace is too long it can be wrapped around the top and tied again in back. Nylon laces will often slip, even with a square knot. The best way I've found to secure them is to take a bight in each lace, shove it through the top eyelet on the opposite side, run the end of the other side through the loop and pull up tight. Nothing can slip this way, yet the arrangement is easy to open.

As mentioned, I wear leather boots in all weather, wet or dry, and I've never found a dressing that will keep water out indefinitely, which means I often have wet feet. I've simply resigned myself to this, preferring water to perspiration. With properly fitting boots and wool socks, it's no problem.

Some Thoughts on Equipment

New boots should be tried on while wearing the socks in which you'll be hunting. And they should be laced up all the way and walked in a bit; both of them, not just one as a typical clerk in a shoe store will try to get you do to. They'll be stiffer when new than after a few weeks of regular wear, but don't count on "breaking in" to eliminate obvious problems. Boots should be comfortable from the first; their leather won't give enough to accommodate for a fit that is really bad.

It's a well known fact that feet swell when much walking is done, and the boot must be of a fit to permit this. However, there is little if any swelling in the heel area; most of it occurs at the ball of the foot, where considerable widening takes place. Therefore, the boot should fit well at the heel, snugly without being tight, and be just a trifle wide in front. The socks will adapt to this, keeping everything full, yet they will compress as the foot swells to make room for its expansion. The foot lengthens, too, after more than normal walking, so the boot should be long enough that no contact is made at the front end. Having your toenails jam up against solid leather can take the pleasure out of walking in a hurry. This shouldn't happen even when walking steeply downhill. When trying boots on, if you can shove your foot far enough ahead to get a finger behind your heel before your big toe makes contact, the length is usually okay.

Just as I like wool socks, I like wool underwear when the weather turns wet and chilly, particularly the long, gray, "itchy, scratchy" kind that Eddie Bauer sells. Under ordinary small game clothing, this provides enough warmth for even winter weather if you're moving (except for extremes such as a Minnesota blizzard howling down out of Canada), yet it isn't as bulky as the quilted kind. It feels better too, warm and natural, with none of the slick, slippery feel of the manmade stuff; that's obnoxious to me when wet, while the wool is just sort of friendly. The ability of wool to preserve warmth even when wet is one of its great values. I've spent many cold, rainy days hunting pheasants, and I've come home soaked to the skin, able to pour water out of each boot and wring great puddles out of my clothing. Yet I've never caught a cold from such activity, and I feel certain my heavy wool underwear deserves the credit here. I wear cotton jockey shorts beneath it, as these can

John Plowman tries to keep dry on a typical late-season ringneck hunt in Pennsylvania.

be changed every day, making it unnecessary to wash the wool suit as often as otherwise would be needed. Two-piece wool suits are available, and they're more convenient, though they tend to be more bulky around the middle where they overlap.

When weather is not bad enough to require wool, I still like cotton long johns because they help protect the legs when the pants ride up crawling over down trees in thick cover, etc.

When I started chasing pheasants, heavy canvas was the usual material for hunting pants, usually double layered in front. I'm still partial to this, but it's hard to find anymore. With the constant push toward lighter weight equipment, manufacturers started turning out pants of closely woven cotton, sometimes called balloon silk, though it's hard to understand where that term came from. That was pretty stuff to get your picture taken in but wasn't worth a hoot in real

The author long ago resigned himself to being soaked to the skin on at least half of the days he hunts, so ignores rain gear and counts on heavy wool underwear and a scalding shower when he gets home to fight off pneumonia. Things were so wet this day that even Ol' Sam lost interest in the birds, once they were taken.

pheasant cover. Following World War II, new tough materials like nylon came along (though many of us didn't get to use them for years as it took so long to wear out our GI equipment), and somewhere along the way the sporting goods manufacturers started to make real improvements in design. Several years ago I gave in to my wife's arguments and got a pair of leather-faced "Brushhunter" pants from the 10-X Company. I have to admit that they're far superior to anything I'd bought or cobbled up for myself in days gone by. Not only does that facing turn briars completely, but the design also takes into account the way the pant leg must slide up when the leg is lifted high, yet it tapers toward the ankle to save weight and eliminate floppiness. A short zipper on the outside bottom of each leg makes it easy to get them on or off over boots. Excellent pants for brush hunting also are available with nylon or Naugahyde facing. These turn brambles well—the nylon seems to slide through the usual hangups with a special sort of slipperyness—and choosing among these three facings becomes a personal decision.

Despite the qualities of such pants, I've found none that are quite perfect. On all I've tried, the facing ends at the top of the thighs, leaving a stretch from there to the belt that's unprotected except for the basic material. This is little barrier to greenbriars or whatever, and in the country I hunt these habitually grow higher than my thighs. I've dealt with the problem by sewing patches of buckskin inside the pant tops, but it would be much simpler if the external facing simply extended to the belt, as it logically should. And since on many occasions brambles wrap around your legs or you have to twist through a tangle backwards and sideways, the facing should extend up the rear of the legs at least to the knees. This would increase the weight and doubtless the price of brush pants somewhat, but when tangled in a mess of thorns, almost unable to move in any direction, the increased cost would seem highly worthwhile.

I realize such suggestions are tending in the direction of all-leather pants, and that these are available. However, I don't think they are really necessary, and the leather-faced models do almost as good a job at much less cost, if the facing is used everywhere it should be. Another alternative would be leather chaps, such as those used by trail riders. This approach may seem extreme to those who think of pheasants as creatures of the fields and swales, but I know

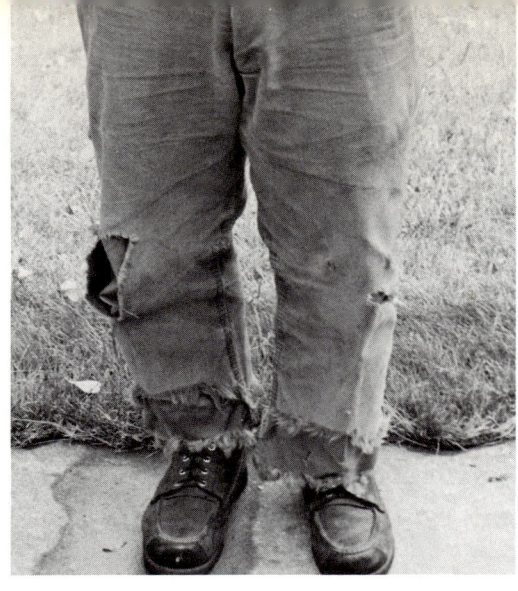

Ordinary hunting pants after a season of booting roosters out of the brambles.

other thick-cover hunters are thinking along the same lines I am, for I saw a gunner using leather chaps during the past season. Waterproof chaps have long been used as protection against rain; why not briarproof ones in the brambles?

No matter what material you prefer in pants, they should be baggy enough not to bind, have deep, strong front pockets for the extra shells you'll carry at times, one hip pocket for a handkerchief and a small folding knife (don't put it in a side pocket where it can get mixed up with the shells and maybe end up in the gun), another for your wallet. The hip pockets should have dependable closures; buttoned flaps are okay, but zippers are better. If you lose your wallet in some briar patch, chances are not too good of finding it, and the loss of all the cards and papers normally stuffed in it can be even more of a nuisance than the money that disappears. A deep watch pocket makes a good place to carry the car keys—and it doesn't hurt to loop a bit of rawhide bootlace through the keyring and onto the belt.

Suspenders do a better job with hunting pants than a belt; or you can follow the old Idaho habit of wearing both. The belt is essentially useless unless a sheath knife is carried. A big knife is unnecessary in small game country, but some guys insist on lugging them. The problem with a belt is that it must be pulled so tightly to keep up the heavy pants, plus the assorted items stuffed in the pockets, that you're likely to give yourself a hernia. Wide suspenders do the job easily and don't interfere with your breathing when you're chasing one of those long-tailed runners.

Some Thoughts on Equipment

Photo taken in early '50s shows same pigskin shirt—which was in better shape then than now! It's been through a lot of briar patches in the seasons since. Cheap felt hat is top choice for pheasant hunting, as it protects ears as well as eyes. Browning sweet sixteen had unaltered 26-inch IC barrel at that time—a fine choice for upland hunting.

With a topnotch dog like Sam to roust birds out of the briars, Jim Bashline doesn't need the armor plating Bell favors, and often chooses nylon-faced pants and light shooting vest over a chamois shirt. Sometimes he suffers.

If the weather is chilly, two shirts are the answer. The inner one should be pure wool of medium to heavy weight. Living in Pennsylvania, I've grown up with the Woolrich brand and haven't the slightest complaint, but you might prefer a Pendleton or whatever. If the temperature is only cool, chamois-cloth material is excellent. It's more comfortable than wool in some ways, particularly around the neck where wool sometimes rubs the skin. (A bandanna tied beneath the collar can help that.) At any rate, this shirt provides the warmth.

Over it I wear a leather shirt. Buckskin is good, but mine happens to be a pigskin job Terry got me from Norm Thompson over twenty years ago. It's heavier than buckskin, durable as iron, and soft as chamois. The thing that leather does better than anything else I know is turn brambles and brush. You can wade through a briar patch that would shred a wool shirt in minutes, yet it doesn't leave a mark on the leather. Not even pigskin lasts forever, and mine is in poor shape now, but I'd have worn out literally dozens of wool shirts in the past couple of decades if I'd tried to bull my way through the places this pigskin shirt has taken me. All in all, it's the best arrangement I've found. I need the protection of a rig like this because I don't like a shooting coat. I wore them for years and the shoulders always bound up on me. Finally I got completely disgusted and went to a shooting vest, but with that you're faced with the problems of briars, Spanish needles, cockleburrs, etc., and only the leather shirt has solved these nuisances for me. If a shooting coat works for you, use it. If not, try the vest-with-leather-shirt approach. The only drawback with leather is water. Mine soaks up rain like a sponge. At times it feels like forty pounds when I pull it off, but it dries soft so I stick with it.

The shooting vest is necessary in the absence of a coat, because you have to have some place to lug your shells and to store whatever birds you shoot. Occasionally I see hunters carrying game on thongs or wire contraptions hooked to their belts, but this looks awfully clumsy, and I don't know what its alleged advantages are. At any rate, a vest provides ample carrying capacity for today's limits, and it doesn't restrict gun swing in the slightest. It doesn't offer much protection against the elements, but it will accommodate enough insulation beneath it to make cold weather no problem. The rain gets to you, but it's possible to wear a rain jacket under it if you like. I've tried that, and as with rubber boots found the perspiration more of a problem than the rain. So now I just accept the fact that I'm going to get wet and ignore it. That's a minor price to pay for the chance to go hunting.

Shooting vests come in several styles and are made of a variety of materials. Some are essentially shooting coats with the sleeves removed, almost of hip length; others are abbreviated so that they scarcely reach the pants belt in front, with an enlarged section in back for carrying game. Practically all of them have loops on the front for shells, usually two rows of six on each side. This is plenty for an average shooting day and makes a particularly convenient way to carry them. This is especially true for double gun shooters who use different loads in each barrel. If shooting 7½s, say, in the right barrel and 6s in the left, you simply keep the 7½s in the loops on the right side of the vest, the 6s on the left side. This makes it unnecessary to look at or sort through assorted shells when reloading. It allows you to maintain top shooting efficiency even when watching the place a downed bird hit the ground. Such separation of shells should be maintained when they are carried in pants pockets, too, of course.

Hunters who use both 12- and 20-gauge guns must be extremely careful not to get their shells mixed up. Most gunners know, but it's

Some Thoughts on Equipment

worth repeating here, that a 20-gauge shell will slide far enough into a 12-gauge barrel that a 12-gauge shell can be chambered behind it. When this happens, and the gun is fired, the best that can be hoped for is a blown-up gun. Depending on precisely where the barrel lets go, and how the pieces take off, you can lose a hand, your eyes, maybe your head. An obstruction near the muzzle, such as mud jammed in by a fall, usually only wrecks the barrel, but a 20-gauge shell lodges a short distance ahead of a 12-gauge chamber and that puts the blowup awfully close to your living parts. It pays to be more than a little bit careful when switching shells in your vest or coat. Years ago I concluded one way to help with this was to get a couple of vests. I shoot the three common gauges, 12-, 16-, and 20-, so I simply got a vest for each gauge. This helps. But I still scrutinize shells closely before loading up for a hunt.

Hats come in all shapes, designs and materials. Anyone who hunts fields exclusively would probably find a broad-brimmed western hat top choice. It has more virtues and fewer faults than anything I've tried, giving excellent protection against sun, snow, and rain. However, it's an impossible choice in the brush or even in ordinary woods. A canvas or leather cap is good here, as the bill gives some protection against glare and many of these have ear tabs that can be pulled down in cold weather. I don't like the plastic-coated models. They keep precipitation off, but they are overly hot. Everything considered, the cheap, crusher-type felt hat is quite likely the best choice for use in all types of cover. It's comfortable, warm enough without being too warm, it clings to the head, and the brim goes all the way around so it protects not only the eyes but also the ears when bulling through the brambles. Its soft material simply folds down over the ears instead of being flipped off as a stiff-brimmed western hat is.

Another necessity is a good pair of gloves. You can get along without these if you avoid the thick places, but as pointed out numerous times earlier, that's where a lot of birds are found, so that's where a hunter eventually winds up. I've found only one suitable type and that's buckskin. They should fit as tightly as your own skin, yet not restrict hand or finger movement in any way. It's possible to achieve this, though it might require that they be made to order. Even so, they aren't real expensive, especially since they last many years in ordinary use. The fingers should be exact length, so you don't get folds of empty leather at the tips just where you want the best fit for proper trigger control. The trigger finger can be cut off the glove—some shooters insist on that—but I haven't found it necessary. Ideally, the gloves should be long enough in the wrist to protect that part of your anatomy when your sleeves slide up as you shove through thick cover with the gun ahead of you. It's hard to find this design, but some taxidermists and leather workers can make them. Quite often, buckskin gloves are built to a design favored by sulky drivers of years past. These have a "bridging" of the palm leather between the first two fingers and thumb, with the surface of the leather rising off the flesh here when the hand is opened. I've been told this was desirable when handling a horse's reins. Maybe so, but I don't like it for gun handling. The leather should be cut so that it clings to the palm no matter what attitude the hand is in.

When of proper design and fit, buckskin gloves cling to the gun even better than the bare hand, particularly when your skin has been wind dried until it's like bone. They of course give excellent protection against briars, thorns, and whatever, and they maintain enough warmth so you can shoot well in all reasonable weather.

Shooting glasses are another item that should be classed as a necessity. The eyes you're born with are the ones you die with, so it pays to give considerable thought to protecting them so they'll last for your lifetime. Large-lensed, heat-treated shooting glasses are the best means of doing this. They keep slapping bushes out of your eyes, protect against occasional stray shot pellets or leaking gas from a defective shell; and if of proper shade and density help you to see better than with the unaided eye, either by reducing glare when it's sunny or providing better contrast between the game and its surroundings when light is poor.

Under bright light conditions, a gray or dark green shade seems best for me, while amber gives best results when natural light is bad. A new design has varying density, in effect "opening up" when the light fails, "darkening up" when it strengthens. I haven't tried these yet but the idea sounds fine.

Neither have I had a chance to try all the makes of shooting glasses. Doubtless all those which have earned good reputations are excellent quality, but I've owned only Bausch & Lomb's Ray-Bans and those from Bushnell and Mitchell. I've used these regularly for many years and they are top quality.

Glasses can be a nuisance in bad weather and I've got to admit that I don't wear them every time I go hunting. But when I don't, I'm aware of their absence, for I know I'm taking unnecessary chances with my eyes. I learned about that the hard way. I once had a varmint rifle blow up when I fired it—without glasses—and spent hours in the hospital having a skilled doctor gently pry bits of brass from the disintegrated case off my eyeballs with a small steel pick. I can tell you truthfully that that isn't an enjoyable way to spend an afternoon. During the following days when I lay quietly in bed, bandages over both eyes, I had plenty of time to think about the pair of Ray-Bans in the gun cabinet that I didn't bother putting on because I was going to fire only one shot. The Good Lord was with me, for when the bandages came off my eyes were okay, but there's no use making Him work overtime when simply wearing a good pair of shooting glasses will eliminate most such problems. So no matter how much you might disagree with my ideas about guns, ammo, boots, or whatever, believe me on this and give serious thought to using properly designed glasses whenever you shoot. It's a helluva lot easier to get a matched pair of Purdeys than another pair of eyes.

Another outstanding development in the field of hunter's safety is the fluorescent orange material used to make caps, vests, and similar items. Clothing made from this highly reflective material is visible under light conditions where all other colors fail. It's an eye-catcher, and because its color is matched by nothing normally appearing in nature, the sight of it instantly warns everyone that a human being is out there, not some strange tree, bird, or animal.

I remember the first time I ever saw fluorescent orange in the woods. It was just after World War II and four of us were camped near Hyner Run in north-central Pennsylvania, deer hunting. I was sitting under a big hemlock on a wet, foggy day, watching some open woods, when I saw a bit of orange moving toward me. It was perhaps 150 yards away when I first saw it, just a glowing spot in the gray sogginess, and I hadn't the slightest idea what it was. But it kept coming closer, like a firefly, and eventually I saw a man under it. The orange spot was his cap. He passed some yards off to my side without seeing me, but for years I wondered where he'd got that orange hat that glowed in the near-dark.

At that time, fresh out of the army, I believed that anyone carrying a gun should be as nearly invisible as possible, so I hunted in OD wool pants dyed forest green and a similar-color parka that L. L. Bean used to sell. That probably was why that orange-capped hunter never noticed me sitting motionless under that hemlock. But after awhile I came to realize that other hunters hadn't the slightest desire to shoot me deliberately, and the best way I could keep them from doing it accidentally was by being as visible as possible. And so when blaze orange items became available—years after that first cap I saw; I don't know what took them so long—I took to wearing them routinely. This feeling was greatly strengthened when I became friends with and a hunting partner of John Behel, hunter safety coordinator for the Pennsylvania Game Commission. His records proved conclusively that my chances of becoming a hunting accident statistic were greatly lessened when fluorescent orange was worn.

It seems to me that anyone with the sense of a goose should recognize the value of orange. All you have to do is look across a dark, foggy ravine where several hunters are moving. Those conventionally clad in canvas or red wool just disappear, while anyone wearing fluorescent orange stands out like a beacon. Some states have made it mandatory to wear a certain minimum number of square inches of orange while hunting. All of them should. Fluorescent orange clothing saves hunters' lives; and even if this fact, in itself, doesn't interest legislators in the slightest, they should also remember that each individual, no matter what else he might be or where his interests might lie, is first and foremost a taxpayer and therefore valuable to a politician!

Awhile back I mentioned preferring a shooting vest to a coat. The design of these makes use of a fluorescent orange vest clumsy. The one simply doesn't fit well over the other and collapses the game pocket. Yet I feel that the orange is necessary. I solved the problem to my satisfaction by cutting up an orange vest to get the material, then sewing strips of it over the shoulder straps and upper front part of the shooting vest and a big piece of it to the upper-back area. This gives me the conspicuousness wanted without the nuisance of an extra vest. Chances are that shooting vests will soon be made of blaze orange material, but until they come along this makeshift arrangement will work.

Pheasants, for most of us, are hunted nearer home than grouse, for they're found in farmlands rather than mountainous areas. Yet few of us can step off our back porches and start after them. This means we must have a way of getting from home to the hunting fields and back. This is no great problem, for if there's anything Americans are familiar with it's cars.

Back in the '20s, most hunters probably did walk from their homes to hunting territory. A far larger percentage of our population was rural then, and life was simpler. In the '30s, which was the midst of the Depression as older hunters will remember, anyone who had any kind of car he could afford to run was doubtless grateful for that privilege, and he used it to go hunting as well as for all other activities where an automobile was necessary. Then came World War II, and that not only put an end to the Depression but also introduced the first utility vehicle which was adaptable to outdoor needs in a way that few hunters had ever dreamed. This of course was the "Quarter-Ton, Four-by-Four, General Purpose Vehicle," which in GI lingo became the "GP" or Jeep.

Though small, cold, and a kidney killer, this iron burro was an instant hit with literally armies of men. Its diminutive size made it maneuverable and let it go places where many larger vehicles just couldn't squeeze, while its four-wheel drive and low-range gearbox gave it the traction and power needed for off-road traveling. It wasn't fast enough for highway use as a steady thing, but most hunters didn't attempt to drive it long distances at high speed, though it isn't uncommon to see one being towbarred to the Rockies from Jersey, say, just to provide transportation during a hunt there. And it isn't unusual to see WWII Jeeps still chugging elk hunters into the high country of Wyoming or Colorado, some thirty years after they left the old Willys factory. The original Jeep is still favored by many western outdoorsmen as its small size lets it go places where today's more powerful, but larger, offspring can't manage. No car should be expected to go on running for three decades, of course, but some of these do. Maybe they're not smart enough to know they're worn out.

The Jeep, which is still following its own evolutionary line, spawned a whole raft of near copies: the British Land Rover, Japanese Toyota Land Cruiser and Nissen Patrol, International Scout, Ford Bronco, Chevrolet Blazer, and others. And the four-wheel drive was made available in an assortment of pickups, station wagons, and other vehicles. All have their virtues and faults, but everything considered they do the job they were intended to do, and all have considerable followings. I have a hunch it's their rugged "male" image that appeals to many hunters, for it's only on extremely rare occasions that the average sportsman ever needs their most popular characteristic, four-wheel drive. Of course, when he does need it, he needs it awfully bad!

At any rate, it's become common for a family to have a second car, one intended primarily for hunting or other "outdoor" use, and quite often this vehicle is a four-wheel drive. I got mine years ago, a Toyota Land Cruiser, and have been driving it daily ever since, both in the city and miles from the nearest hardtop, on short jaunts around town and on hunting trips out of the country. It's got an awful lot of miles on it, and I'm hoping to add a lot more. It doesn't ride like a Cadillac, but I've driven it 750 miles between breakfast and bedtime without undue fatigue, and when necessary it's taken me through swamps and up trackless, overgrown mountains where a Caddie wouldn't get fifty yards. So you pay your money and take your choice, as with guns, dogs, and everything else.

The short wheelbase rigs don't have a lot of luggage room, but can usually manage several hunters and their guns, dogs, and equipment on the normal length hauls that put them into hunting country. If desired, this equipment can include dry clothing and shoes to slip into after a wet day afield. This often is mentioned in hunting books of a few decades ago, and the idea would seem to have merit. Yet I rarely bother. With today's highways, most one-day hunting jaunts are within an hour's drive or so of home, so I just don't make the effort to change into dry socks and shoes, no matter how soaked my feet are. The car heater flows right on them and that, plus my wool socks, make things reasonably comfortable. The game vest is shed, of course, and if my leather shirt is really soaked through, I pull it off and slip on a dry warm jacket that was left in the Land Cruiser. In ordinary

Some Thoughts on Equipment

temperatures, the top of a set of dacron-insulated underwear is fine for this; if the weather is really cold, a goosedowned jacket is unbeatable.

The guns can be a nuisance in a Jeep-type vehicle. Holding them is inconvenient—practically impossible for the driver—and there just isn't any place to lay them. Best solution I know is to install racks. In a pickup this normally goes above and behind the seat, but I dislike this as it displays them to everyone in the rear window, which can cause a reaction among hunter-haters and can attract thieves when you're in a lunchroom or whatever. In the Toyota I put a three-gun rack behind the front seat. This keeps them out of the way yet readily available, and they're out of sight from most angles. Some units carry a pair of guns along the front of a pickup seat, behind the occupants' lower legs. I've never tried that but it seems like a good idea.

It's simple to carry extra shells, lunches, hot coffee, tea, or chocolate, and anything else that might be needed in a normal day's hunt. When the weather is hot, as it often is early in the season, I stop at one of the roadside stands common in southeastern Pennsylvania where I do most of my pheasant hunting and buy a gallon of cider. It's sold in plastic containers, which means there's no problem with breakage, and the taste is more satisfying than water for it quenches better.

10

Why I Hunt

"Why do you hunt?" the gray-haired lady opposite me at the dining table asked, her eyes serious behind light-reflecting pince-nez glasses, her voice showing a trace of honest puzzlement. "How can anyone, in this day and age, justify hunting down and shooting other living creatures? How can you deliberately *kill* something?"

Questions like these come much more often now than in decades past, probably because of the change from rural to urban life which has taken most of our population out of contact with the basic facts of life, those which naturally illustrate that life depends on death. A hunter's first reaction to such questions is often a purely emotional one—anger. His hackles rise at the first inkling that someone is going to debate his right to do something that he's enjoyed perhaps since he was a boy. Why do they even have a right to ask such things? he wonders, and sometimes his feelings are so intense that he either snarls a reply, walks angrily away, or stands mute, refusing even to engage in conversation.

Yet such questions deserve answers. Most of the persons asking them have no idea why a hunter hunts. If they knew, they wouldn't ask. Admittedly, it was the anti-hunters who brought up most such questions in the first place, or, more accurately, opposed hunting so vociferously that otherwise uninterested persons became curious. Many of this latter group are at least willing to ask the hunter's views, for which we should be grateful. The anti-hunters rarely, if ever, ask questions of persons who might give them a reply; they prefer to make their questions rhetorical: "How could anyone shoot a gentle brown-eyed deer?"; "Why is anyone so callous that he can kill and eat an innocent, brown-eyed baby rabbit?" And so on, and so on, *ad infinitum, ad nauseam.*

I reply to the questions in various ways, depending on my mood of the moment, who the questioner is, etc. If it's someone obnoxious, I might answer the first question literally: "I center my crosshairs tight behind the shoulder, preferably so the bullet will catch both lungs, and squeeze the trigger." This just antagonizes them more, of course, but that's the most you can hope for with some persons. Sometimes the old Yankee trait of answering one question with another is useful: "How can you sit across the table from me and obviously enjoy a sirloin steak that just a few days ago was part of a living, breathing, brown-eyed Angus steer?" Or even more pathetic ". . .a chop that was carved off the cadaver of a happy, gamboling, innocent, brown-eyed, little lamb?"

Those innocent, brown eyes work both ways, you see. And sometimes, suddenly realizing what that means, a dinner companion comes close to losing her cookies. (Or his; a lot of the little old ladies who criticize hunters are biologically males.) You can see the queasiness come up behind their eyes, watch the tightening of the mouth, the stiffening of the throat muscles, when they have to face the fact that the perfectly broiled steak they've just sliced up on their plates, chewed with great gusto, and swallowed, was not too long ago an honest-to-God living creature, one with eyes that saw, a nose that smelled, and a brain that had certain mental capabilities. This can be a traumatic experience for a person who wanted only to slip it in the hunter and break it off, but now he somehow finds himself equally guilty of whatever crime or sin he thought was the gunner's alone. And it serves him right, so far as I'm concerned. Such holier-than-thou types give me a roaring pain. It's never enough for them to take care of their own lives, they're not happy unless they're running everyone else's too.

I doubt if there's much point in talking to or about the anti-hunters, though. For whatever reasons, their minds are made up. They're against hunting now, will be against fishing in the future, and doubtless will oppose golf, table tennis, or sex when the mood strikes them.

The uncommitted group—which makes up about ninety percent of the non-hunting population—is the one with which we should be concerned. These are the people who have no personal interest in this situation and, being emotionally uninvolved, are willing to listen to both sides of the argument. They also are the ones who, because of sheer numbers, have the political clout to make their feelings known, and thus are the ones to whom we should make our position known. Hunters must come to realize that in the end, whether we like it or not, it's politics that determines whether we will hunt, or where and when it will or will not be done. This is an area that most of us would rather avoid, but if we don't get involved, preferably as a group as that carries the most weight with legislators, we'll find our rights frittered away one by one, until finally there won't be enough left with which to bother. To think this can't happen is foolish; worse than that, it's stupid. Just compare the situation of the average hunter today with that of his father and see how much we've lost in but a few years. This trend, projected into the future a generation or two, gives a prospect that's frightening.

The truth of the matter is—and this is what we should explain to the uncommitted—there is no reason to be ashamed of hunting, no reason not to enjoy this sport in a legitimate manner. It's an activity that dates back to the beginning of mankind; even earlier, actually, if we consider our predecessor species. Just considering ourselves, we can look back more than a million years, perhaps as much as ten million years, to the time when some kind of man took some kind of weapon, a club, a rock, maybe an animal bone, and went out and clobbered some sort of critter and brought it home for his family to eat. That man was one of our ancestors. He was a hunter, and because he hunted well, you and I and everyone else in this world are alive. We exist only because from time immemorial our ancestors survived by hunting. They gathered wild food too, fruits and berries, seeds and roots, and they probably fished some, though that was a more difficult thing to do at that time, but basically they were hunters. They lived off the animals which lived off the land.

It wasn't until about 10,000 or 15,000 years ago that agriculture had its beginnings. That's a long time when one thinks in terms of a human life span, but it's only a drop in the bucket when related to man's total time on earth. *Homo sapiens* has been a farmer, at most, for perhaps one percent of his span here, and maybe only a tenth of that. For at least 99 percent of his time on earth, man has been first and foremost a hunter.

With an ancestry like that, stretching back into the mists of time, so far back that our only remaining physical links are mere bits of bones and stone, I don't think it's at all absurd or anachronistic that many of us still are hunters. The same genes that helped our ancestors survive are still in us today. We may use them for other goals now, to compete for jobs or success or money or whatever, but basically those drives and instincts are still the same, and some of us, compelled by these ancient forces, still hunt animals as our forefathers of perhaps half a million generations ago did. We don't do it for precisely the same reasons. We don't have to kill wild animals for food now. We can buy the meat of tame animals that others have raised and slaughtered and processed for us, and that's progress, you see. We just do it because there's something in our blood that drives us.

That's the part that shocks and offends some people. They say we should have progressed beyond that stage, that the recent 10,000 years of living off agriculture should have banished it from our blood; that we should have no urge to kill for ourselves, but should live like civilized beings off the crops of the farmer and the force-fed, plastic-wrapped supermarket meat of the butcher. But I say these people can't face facts. They are talking about a way they believe people *should* feel and act. I'm talking about the way they *do* act.

Man is a hunter and there are many reasons why he hunts: to feel a closeness to nature; to renew a spiritual relationship to the earth from which he sprang; to see a natural beauty that has vanished from too many places. Sometimes just to get away from other people for a little while, even from his own family no matter how much he loves them.

But there is more to hunting than this. Hunting also means closing in on a living creature and killing it. It means personally taking some animal's life. There is no escaping this. Without the

In the final analysis, it's the hunter's ability and willingness to kill that sets him apart from other outdoors-oriented persons. Yet it isn't necessary for him to kill anything in order to have a completely satisfying day afield; in fact, many hunters pass up game they could legally take. However, the hunter knows that his legal harvest of game is a natural and legitimate function. He also knows it is his contribution that makes it possible for our large game populations to exist today.

intent to kill, and the means to do it, there is no real hunting. We might as well go for a hike in the woods. But a hike in the woods does not satisfy a man who is a hunter, at least not during that part of the year he now calls hunting season. The act is only complete and fully satisfying when he actually kills and brings home to his family a bird or animal which he wants to use as food, or takes a trophy that has challenged him. Admittedly, many times he comes home empty-handed, but that is due to lack of opportunity or ability, not lack of desire. Or it may come about after a man has hunted many years and proved to himself that he can bag game if he wants to. He then will often pass up shots he could make, perhaps because they don't challenge his skill enough, perhaps because he somehow feels he has killed enough in his time. But even such a hunter will normally kill on occasion, if only to reassure himself of his efficiency.

A few moments ago I said that everyone now alive has descended from hunting ancestors. This might not be true. I like to say it is, because it strengthens my arguments and embarrasses those who violently oppose hunting, obviously we have no way of being certain about this. However, man has hunted all through history. It was a respected, even honored, activity. The great castles of Europe are hung with trophies of the chase, and most members of the ruling classes took part routinely. Many still do. In fact, in some areas of the world, it's only the so-called upper classes that are permitted to hunt.

Things are different in the United States. From our very beginning we've had a tradition of recognizing the rights of the common man. Actually, the political rulers recognized these rights because they had no choice; the so-called common man of our frontier days, a fiercely independent and self-reliant creature, simply appropriated certain rights which his European peers had lost centuries before (if they ever had them) and successfully resisted any efforts to limit these to certain groups.

One of the things the U.S. citizen had the opportunity to do, since before this country became a nation, was hunt. When the white man arrived on this continent, there was wild game like he'd never dreamed of in Europe, and it was his for the taking. He didn't have to be a king or a nobleman to take part, all he had to do was get a gun and go.

Well, he got his gun and he went. And the wild critters, the deer and the buffalo and the antelope, the elk and the sheep and the bears, fed him while he tamed a continent. It's easy for us to look back now and criticize him, for by today's standards he was a ruthless slaughterer. But in his time and place, that early hunter—what we often call a market hunter now, but which for the most part was the farmer or the rancher with a big family to feed and an apparently inexhaustible resource to utilize—that hunter was a natural or normal phenomenon. Wilderness was something to be conquered; game was something put on earth to feed him.

By 1887, little more than a century after we won our independence from England, the American buffalo, the bison, had vanished from our plains; almost no whitetails were left in Pennsylvania; there were less than a half-million deer in all of the U.S. By the first decade of this century, perhaps only 50,000 elk remained, and there were less than 25,000 antelope. Today's hunters are still blamed for these killings in some sort of guilt by tenuous association. The truth is, many of those earlier hunters actually thought their supplies were limitless, while others believed that wild game had to go to make room for more useful domesticated animals. It is hard to picture a midwestern farmer of today trying to raise corn and wheat in fields that herds of buffalo might periodically wander through. It's also hard to figure how the small army detachments of our frontier days would ever have defeated the plains Indians if the buffalo hadn't been taken from them. That one animal provided everything the Indian needed in the way of food, shelter, and clothing, and the Indian, the greatest guerilla fighting force that ever existed, wasn't defeated until the buffalo was gone. This is not to say I condone the slaughter of any species, but we should try to examine the events of those days from the viewpoint of the persons who were then living and involved.

Our big game was on the verge of extinction, and there were danger signs in some small game populations when, in 1901, Teddy Roosevelt became president. So far as wildlife was concerned, his arrival was the U.S. Cavalry pounding up in the last reel, bugles blaring and guns blasting. It's frightening to think what our situation might be today if we'd got a typical politician at that time instead of old Teddy, who actually was pretty young then.

Teddy Roosevelt established the U.S. Forest Service, increased the national forest acreage from 33 million to 140 million acres, and, just as important, conceived the idea of "conservation through wise use." This is the real core of wildlife management. Roosevelt and his chief forester, Gifford Pinchot, came to recognize that wildlife and forests were *renewable* resources that would last forever if properly managed and utilized. This is the point that many of today's anti-hunters still don't recognize. They think wildlife can and should be stockpiled to increase its future numbers, or that it will just stabilize itself at some nice acceptable level, giving them something to admire on an autumn evening. Wildlife and nature don't work that way.

But back at the turn of the century, game was scarce, and to put the market hunter out of business the Lacey Act was passed in 1900. This said no game taken illegally could be transported across state lines. This was followed in 1918 by the Migratory Bird Treaty Act, signed by Canada and the U.S., which put migratory game and birds under custody of the federal government. This eventually established the principle that waterfowl hunting was no longer the unregulated right of citizens but was a privilege to be enjoyed as the law permitted. In other words, the principles of seasons and bag limits were established. Hunting was for sport now, not for the market.

Some people object even to sport hunting, fearing this will cause the extermination of a species, and when not much is known about wildlife, the obvious solution to any problem seems to be "protection." We get that word today from the newly aroused ecologists. Protect whatever species you're interested in and soon everything will be just fine, they say. People thought the same thing early in this century too, and they learned it doesn't work. Life isn't that simple, and complete protection can be the worst thing possible for wildlife. Various examples prove this. Perhaps the most famous one is the deer herd of Arizona's Kaibab region, that strip north of the Grand Canyon and south of Utah. Teddy Roosevelt made this the Grand Canyon National Game Preserve in 1906. The predators were largely eliminated and hunting was not permitted. By 1924, the 3000 deer that had been there had increased to over 100,000. The food supply had been destroyed, and deer were dying by the tens of thousands. Within a few years, the herd was down to about 15,000, and the range was ruined. It took decades for it to restore itself.

A similar thing happened in my home state of Pennsylvania. Deer were practically extinct here at the turn of the century. A few were stocked, and they were protected. Newly logged-off regions supplied good browse, bucks only were hunted, and the population took off. Currently, Pennsylvania's deer herd numbers well over 600,000, and sport hunters harvest some 125,000 annually. The only way deer can truly be managed is through antlerless deer seasons regulated by the Game Commission. Hunting bucks only will not keep the herd in control. Deer are polygamous, each mature doe usually has twins, and under average conditions it takes only two or three breeding seasons to double a herd in size. If you start with about 650,000 deer, as now exist in this state, and completely protect them, there theoretically could be eight or ten million in less than a dozen years. But the range would be long gone before that point was reached, along with the farmers' crops and the shrubbery in the suburbs, and starvation would have wiped out most of the herd. This is why Pennsylvania and some other states must have antlerless deer seasons, and one reason we can't afford to let the anti-gun and anti-hunting people have their way.

Many such groups advocate letting these animals starve (a real kind-hearted approach!) suggesting that will bring everything into some sort of "balance of nature." But that's nothing more than a miserable catch phrase to describe a condition that never truly existed and never will. The anti-hunting groups seem to think that at some certain point everything in the world is in some state of equilibrium, that everything is peaches and cream, that everybody's a brother. It isn't and never was and never will be. Nature doesn't give a damn about anything at all, really. "Nature" is just a word for an overall condition or situation in which everything exists—including humans. We are not something separate from and superior to all others life forms. We are just another part of the whole. Whether any species continues or vanishes means nothing to nature. In the long run, the only plants and animals that succeed are those that struggle successfully for what they want. All things eventually vanish; even the seemingly successful ones, for their success, too, is only temporary.

A half century ago the overall wildlife picture in this country was not good, and a majority of our population was ready to give up on it and get on with furthering the advance of "civilization." However, in the late '20s, a group called "The American Game Association," a few conservationists who believed in constructive work, held its first annual public meeting to deal with wildlife problems. Among those attending were Aldo Leopold, Seth Gordon, John C. Phillips, and A. Willis Robertson. The outcome of this group's work was a game policy stressing the *productive phase* of wildlife management, as compared with the *restrictive phase* that earlier had been advocated. The goal was to study wildlife scientifically and to set up programs that would maintain it as a viable resource. Researchers in Iowa talked of a "biological balance" law, that condition in which all losses to a given game population are compensated for by natural reproduction, with fish and game being *managed* to maintain this situation. Studies such as this require wildlife biologists, money, land, and a way of contacting scientists in related fields. Subsidized by the Sporting Arms and Ammunition Manufacturers Institute, cooperative wildlife research units were set up in various states' land grant colleges in the mid '30s. The federal government later added its help. Eighteen research units are at work today. These provide much of the data in the field of wildlife management.

Programs like this have one great need: money. License fees can't pay the whole tab. In 1933 the federal government had imposed a 10% excise tax on sporting arms and ammunition. This went into the treasury. It was not earmarked for any specific purpose. Senator Key Pittman of Nevada, chairman of the Commission on Conservation of Wildlife Resources, claimed that if gasoline taxes could be earmarked for road building, gun and ammo taxes could be assigned to game habitat building. He got the support of the sportsmen and introduced a bill in the senate, while Representative A. Willis Robertson of Virginia sponsored a similar bill in the house. In 1937, the Pittman-Robertson Federal Aid in Wildlife Restoration Act became law. It allocates the excise tax on guns and ammunition to the states on the basis of land area and hunting license buyers. Since 1937, some $500,000,000 have resulted from the Pittman and Robertson program. This money is used to purchase land for wildlife, to develop land for wildlife, for investigations and surveys to improve administration of wildlife resources, and to coordinate projects necessary to efficient management of wildlife resources.

It's interesting to note that sportsmen asked to have this tax continued some years back, when similar excise taxes were being dropped. It's also interesting to note that, despite all the malarkey that the anti-hunters put out, not one of their groups comes up with any money to actually help wildlife. It's only the hunters, the guys with guns who are looked on as cold-blooded killers by the so-called friends of animals, who actually pay to maintain a wildlife program in this country.

The anti-hunters argue that we have a selfish motive in this, that we support wildlife programs only in order to have game to shoot. That's true to some extent, but at least we do support the programs, and as a result we for many years have had viable wildlife populations in areas where they would have been long gone if their re-establishment and survival had to depend upon anyone else. Wildlife management programs financed by hunters' money and designed and carried out by trained game biologists have built up many populations to greater levels than they were before the white man set foot on this continent. As mentioned earlier, there were less than a half million deer in the entire country in the last decade of the 19th Century. Pennsylvania alone now has far more than this, some 650,000, and the U.S. whitetail deer population totals perhaps 10 million. There are millions more mule deer and blacktails. The elk population has tripled in this century, despite the fact that its range had been severely restricted, with much of it harmed by domestic animal usage. Wild turkeys exist in large numbers in many states—large enough numbers to justify both spring and fall seasons in some—and there is a good black bear population. The pronghorn antelope provides excellent hunting in many western states. Wyoming's annual harvest normally exceeds the total number of pronghorns in the U.S. at the turn of the century. And of course the pheasant has made its home here, providing an annual crop of many

Hunting often creates deep companionships that don't arise from any other human activity. Hunting was probably the first cooperative venture men took part in, and it might well be the last.

millions. All of this is due to the hunter's money and efforts. The anti-hunters, so long on talk and loud in criticism, do absolutely nothing of a constructive nature to aid wildlife. Viewed from any objective standpoint, it's obvious that in this world it's the hunter who is the true conservationist, while the new self-proclaimed animal-lover is no more than a loud noise.

Many side benefits accrue to non-hunters from the hunter's efforts, too. Millions of acres purchased with and supported by hunting license money also make it possible for dozens of non-game species to exist in good numbers, species which bring pleasure to bird watchers, hikers, and others who enjoy the out of doors but do not hunt. Such outdoorsmen should give thought to what they'll be losing if hunting is legislated out of existence and these vast territories lose the support of the license dollar. For these areas to survive without the hunter, monies will have to come from increased taxation and bureaucracy, a situation that few persons enjoy contemplating.

The anti-hunting movement is particularly depressing when one realizes that the whole thing boils down to a moral judgment on the part of a few self-appointed censors. The most superficial observation of life on this planet proves that everything lives off of something else. Herbivores eat the plants which grow in the ground and gain their sustenance from it. The carnivores eat the herbivores, and some critters eat anything that grows, walks, flies, or rots. The whole thing is a never-ending circle, and we're part of it. That's how it's been since life began, and that's how it'll be until this old world becomes a burned out cinder and slowly dissolves into dust that scatters and drifts into nothingness throughout the universe. It's understandable how every now and again some holier-than-thou souls take it on themselves to try to change human nature. There are aberrant individuals in all species, but nature has a way of eliminating them before too long. I can have sympathy for some of them; for instance, the person who believes that he should not eat any living creature and makes a hundred percent effort to live as a vegetarian. He's unsuccessful, of course, as a microscopic study of the water he drinks will prove, but his intentions are genuine and I respect him. However, I've never met an anti-hunter who was even a half-time vegetarian, so I can't believe their arguments are sincere. They feel it's all right for them to eat beef or pork or lamb or whatever, but they don't feel it's all right for the person who is going to eat the meat to kill it. They would rather have that done by someone offstage. They want to be so far removed from the actual act that they don't have to live with the knowledge that it ever occurred. A plastic-wrapped supermarket steak, to their minds, is just an item of food. They see no direct connection between it and a living animal. If they should happen to consider this, they feel no connection with the animal's death because that was carried out by some faceless man whose job it is to do such things. That's what makes meat eating and animal killing acceptable to them: the fact that it satisfies their appetites, and someone else does the dirty work for money. Then it's just a job, a way for somebody to make a living. But they do object to my killing animals for sport or food. With no legal justification for their feelings, they render a moral judgment on my actions.

I object to their objections. I don't believe anyone has the right to make me conform to his wishes in a situation like this.

Earlier I said that many hunters feel anger when someone questions their actions, and many times this is my own reaction. After I cool down a bit, however, or when the person I'm talking to is not belligerent but merely curious about my sport, I find my primary emotion is sadness. My sadness is not only for the beleaguered position held by the hunters but also for those millions of persons who have never known the satisfaction that comes from hunting. Just think of the experiences, the fulfillments, the joys, and the sorrows that your hunting has brought you. Then stop and consider for a moment the fact that most of the persons now living, and most of those yet to be born, will never share in such days as you and I have known.

It's said you can't miss what you've never had. But how empty a non-hunting man's life must be when the years come on and he sits alone and looks back.

On a long winter's evening, when the wind howls round the eaves and the hard snow rattles off the panes, the hunter sprawls in his old sag-bottom chair, luxuriously fatigued by hills he wouldn't have noticed as a youngster but satisfied that in his life he'd met their

Some men and some animals are born to hunt. There are worse things they could do.

challenge, staring into the flames, smelling the woodsmoke from birch and hickory and hearing the occasional tick of a dropping ember, half-empty glass forgotten in his hand, looking back to perhaps that first early morning of his youth when he followed his dad up a briar-grown ravine, little shotgun cradled in his arms, brand new boots scuffling through frost-stiffened swale grass and breath clouds hanging in the air—going rabbit hunting! Just as the sun's bright disc broke the horizon, the pealing of beagles came, more beautiful than distant bells, and the sudden pounding of his heart sent the blood coursing so rapidly through his veins that his cheeks burned like fire despite the November chill! Lord, what a day that was. A half century can pass but every detail of that dawn will still be vivid in his mind's eye, and because his little 20-gauge sent the scuttling rabbit cartwheeling through the frozen weeds and he took it home and because his mother cooked it, that cottontail lives on, and it will till the day he dies, immortalized in his memory instead of being ignominiously flattened by the wheels of an automobile or speared by the talons of a hungry hawk.

What does the non-hunter remember when his time is short and old friends are gone?

Later on, the hunter recalls, prowling that damp, crushed-grape-smelling hollow he found alone. He eased his way through the tangled vines, waded the shallow creek, and climbed the steep opposite hillside, only to be brought to a sudden halt by the heart-jamming thunder of a flushing grouse. Clutching a swaying sapling in one hand, gun in the other, one foot waving free in the air, its purchase collapsed beneath him, he hung helpless as the bird vanished. Many's the grouse that humiliated him in later years, but none more thoroughly than that first one he put out while carrying a gun.

He has many other memories. The golden days of October with the maples like splashes of fire on the hills. Their colors were rivaled only by the flashing long-tailed bird that squawked its way upward, feathers glittering in the sunlight, and curved away to vanish like an arrow. The sweltering days of September; the sky a cloudless, colorless bowl that concentrated the heat like a gigantic oven, while he stood motionless in the scant shade of a fencerow flanking the tall standing corn, the wide green leaves dulled by dust, watching, waiting, for the mourners he knew would come with the lengthening shadows. Sweat dribbling down his temples, camouflage jacket as impermeable to ventilation as a plastic sheet, boots slowly curling his toes into quivering masses of athlete's foot, he waited. And then they came—thin, gray streaks against the sky, flickering in and out of sight like squirts of quicksilver—and his autoloader dully boomed three times, and he watched disconsolately as they disappeared, unscathed, in the distance.

Sometimes, he remembers, you didn't die of the heat; sometimes you froze. In a duck blind, for instance, the moist cold seeping through goosedown underwear, feet slowly congealing into two big ice cubes, while you stubbornly waited out that last flight that might give you a chance to drop just one more mallard so you'd have enough for Thanksgiving dinner. Waves lapped endlessly against the blind; then, finally, there was the sound of wings above. When he raised his head above the gray-painted box, the sleet hit his face like gravel, and when he flung off a glove and shouldered the gun, the metal bit fast to the flesh. But that wasn't enough to keep him from swinging past the vague hen silhouettes to pick up the front greenhead and drop him among the decoys.

Cold is different on a deer trail. The big woods are silent, bitter in late afternoon, and the road hunters are far behind. Only the pointed dimples in the snow lead onward, across a windswept field into black pines. Cheeks stiff and raw from the wind, watering eyes straining, he moves around the field in a wide half-circle, silent but hurrying, racing the lowering sun he can't see behind the gray clouds. A quarter-mile beyond the field he stops beneath a large hemlock to watch a flat that stretches along the ridge angling rearward. Minutes later a dark shadow catches his eye against dull whiteness. It's the buck. It's clearly visible in the field of his scope, and a well-placed shot ends his hunt. He field-dresses the animal quickly, fastens his drag rope and leans into it. It's a long way to the Jeep, and night is near....

Looking back, it dawns on him that experiences such as these illustrate much of the difference between the hunter and the hiker, between those with true survival instincts—the killer mentality and ability—and the dilettantes whose appreciation of the outdoors fades as the temperature drops and the weather worsens. The hunter meets nature on its own terms, its worst as well as its best, and he takes primitive joy in the battle. Sometimes he wins, sometimes he loses—sometimes he even dies—but a group of blood-brother hunters survives to perpetuate the instinct that dates back to the beginning and hopefully will last as long as anything in this world is worth fighting for.

Was agriculture the big mistake? the man muses. The hunter-fisherman-food gatherer existed for millions of years in harmony with the earth, a part of it, belonging to it, living off its natural surpluses, harming nothing. But with agriculture came this exploding population, a population which in scarcely 10,000 years has grown to literally number billions—all actually living an artificial existence, for almost every life ultimately depends on the earth's few inches of topsoil, and that topsoil is wearing out.

We followed the wrong fork in the trail, the man decides. Trading the hunter's bow for the farmer's plow was the greatest error in mankind's history. But it isn't necessarily fatal. Our hunting instinct could, at some future time, be the salvation of the human race.

Other thoughts slip in as the fire burns lower and the shadows thicken. Memories of Maine's pine woods, Pennsylvania's hardwood

slashings, Arizona's deserts, Colorado's mountains, Idaho's timberline country, the black spruce and blue lakes of Ontario and Quebec. Even as he conjures up the magic, never-to-be-forgotten remembrances of those days and places, somewhere on the edge of his consciousness he hears that strident voice again demand, "Why do you hunt?"

He stiffens in anger, then slowly relaxes. "You poor soul," he murmers. "You poor miserable soul. Why can't you understand that the real question is, *'Why don't you hunt?'* "

Works Consulted

Complete Book of Rifles and Shotguns, by Jack O'Connor, Harper and Row, New York City, 1961.
Game Shooting, by Robert Churchill, rev. by Macdonald Hastings, Stackpole Co., Harrisburg, Pa., 1967.
The Modern Shotgun, 3 vols., by Major Gerald Burrard, Charles Scribner's Sons, New York City, 1931-32.
New Hunter's Encyclopedia, 3rd ed., Stackpole Co., Harrisburg, Pa., 1966.
Pheasants in North America, ed. by Durward L. Allen, Stackpole Co., Harrisburg, Pa., 1956.
Pheasants: Their Lives and Homes, by William Beebe, published under the auspices of the New York Zoological Society by Doubleday, Page and Co., Garden City, N.Y., 1926.
Ring-Necked Pheasant, 2nd ed., by John Madson, Olin Mathieson Chemical Co., East Alton, Ill., 1963.
Ruffed Grouse, by John Madson, Winchester Press, East Alton, Ill., 1969.
Sure-Hit Shotgun Ways, by Francis Sell, Stackpole Co., Harrisburg, Pa., 1967.
Winchester Ammunition Handbook, 6th ed., Olin Mathieson Chemical Co., New Haven, Conn.

I want to express my special thanks to Fred Hartman, a wildlife biologist who has worked with and studied pheasants for many years, for his comments and advice on Chapters Two and Three.

The photos in this book were taken during a number of different hunting seasons by quite a few different persons, and unfortunately it isn't possible to give precise credit for each one. Most of the action shots were taken by Joe Osman, who handles a camera as I'd like to handle a gun, with a few by another pro, Ralph Cady, several by Sylvia Bashline, and the remainder by unknown but not forgotten hunting pals.

The dust-cover painting is by another friend, Taylor Oughton, who understands and can show the electric excitement at the moment of truth when a couple of these long-tailed birds flush.